1 MONTH OF
FREE
READING

at

www.ForgottenBooks.com

By purchasing this book you are eligible for one month membership to ForgottenBooks.com, giving you unlimited access to our entire collection of over 1,000,000 titles via our web site and mobile apps.

To claim your free month visit:

www.forgottenbooks.com/free913076

ISBN 978-0-265-94085-3
PIBN 10913076

LEAGUE OF LIBRARY COMMISSIONS

HAND - BOOK

COMPILED BY

CLARA F. BALDWIN

SECRETARY MINNESOTA PUBLIC LIBRARY COMMISSION

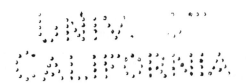

PRINTED FOR THE

LEAGUE OF LIBRARY COMMISSIONS

December, 1910

CONTENTS.

Introductory note 3
Historical Summary 5
League of Library Commissions 12
    Publications 15
    Constitution 17
Organization and Activities of Commissions 20
    Alabama Dept. of Archives and History 20
    California State Library 22
    Colorado State Board of Library Commissioners 25
    Colorado Traveling Library Commission 26
    Connecticut Free Public Library Committee 27
    Delaware State Library Commission 30
    Georgia Library Commission 31
    Idaho State Library Commission 32
    Illinois Library Extension Commission 33
    Indiana Public Library Commission 34
    Iowa Library Commission 38
    Kansas Traveling Libraries Commission 41
    Kentucky Library Commission 42
    Maine Library Commission 44
    Maryland State Library Commission 45
    Massachusetts Free Public Library Commission 46
    Michigan State Board of Library Commissioners 48
    Minnesota Public Library Commission 50
    Missouri Library Commission 55
    Nebraska Public Library Commission 57
    New Hampshire Public Library Commission 59
    New Jersey Public Library Commission 60
    New York State Education Department:—
        Division of Educational Extension 62
    North Carolina Library Commission 66
    North Dakota Public Library Commission 68
    Ohio Board of Library Commissioners 70
    Oregon Library Commission 73
    Pennsylvania Free Library Commission 79
    Rhode Island Department of Education:—
        State Committee on Libraries 81
    Tennessee Free Library Commission 83
    Texas Library and Historical Commission 84
    Utah Library-Gymnasium Commission 85
    Vermont Board of Library Commissioners 87
    Virginia State Library 91
    Washington State Library Commission 92
    Wisconsin Free Library Commission 94
Directory of Library Commissions 102

INTRODUCTORY NOTE.

Three editions of the Yearbook of Library Commissions' were published by the League in 1906, 1907 and 1908.

The annual publication will now be discontinued, and the present *Handbook* follows the plan of previous *Yearbooks* in its effort to furnish in convenient form information regarding the organization and work of each commission. All statistical tables have been omitted from this edition, as it is proposed to issue annual supplements giving statistics for the year, with notes regarding new commissions organized, or important new work undertaken by any commission.

Grateful acknowledgment is herewith extended to the officers of the various commissions who have furnished material on the work in their respective states.

C. F. B.

284284

HISTORICAL SUMMARY.

With the recent growth of the library extension movement, and the recognition of the public library as an "integral part of public education," has developed the idea of fostering and encouraging this movement by state aid or supervision in some form. The public school systems of our several states have been brought to their present successful operation through generous state aid and encouragement, and the public library systems are now claiming equal recognition as educational institutions. In spite of the fact that statistics show a great increase in the number of books accessible to the people, a careful study of conditions in rural communities shows that many millions of people have no access to libraries. To solve this problem of furnishing free books to the entire population, the aid of the state has naturally been sought. Another problem of library extension is that of the small library with small income and inexperienced service. To encourage a healthful growth in such libraries and promote their efficiency, the need of some center of information is apparent.

Thirty-five states are now undertaking library extension work, twenty-five through library commissions, seven through the state library, and three under the direction of the state department of education. Although the organization and methods of the several states differ materially, the common aim is to encourage the establishment of libraries in all communities able to support them, to promote the efficiency of libraries already established and in 29 states to maintain a system of traveling libraries to aid in solving the problem of making free books accessible to all the people.

Massachusetts was the first state to establish a library commission, although Rhode Island claims priority in library extension work, since it began to give state aid to free public libraries for the purchase of books in 1875. The Massachusetts Commission, established in 1890, was authorized to grant to any town upon the establishment of a free public library, $100. in books to be selected by the Commission. When the law was enacted there were 105 towns out of 352 without free libraries, and Massachusetts now has the distinction of being the only state in the union which has a public library in every town.

New Hampshire followed the next year, 1891, by enacting a law nearly identical with the Massachusetts law, which gives $100 to each town founding a free library. The New Hampshire Commission was instrumental in passing a compulsory library law, according to which every town must levy a certain assessment to maintain a library; the minimum amount instead of the maximum is prescribed; if the town has no library, the fund accumulates; and if a town wishes to omit an assessment, it must especially vote to do so. In 1903, the Board of Library Commissioners was abolished, and the work turned over to the trustees of the State Library, who have assumed all the duties and powers of the former commission.

In 1892, New York entered the list, developing a system of state supervision of libraries with more complete centralization than has yet been attempted in any other state. The work has been done by the Home Education Division of the University of the State of New York, the director of the State Library being also director of Home Education, so that the two interests have been identified. Under the law, the regents of the University were given power to issue charters and give financial aid to libraries which fulfilled certain conditions. These libraries are supervised and inspected yearly, and two organizers now give their entire time to the work of visiting and assisting libraries. New York was the first state to establish traveling libraries, the first libraries being sent out in 1893.

The library school is also under the direction of the Department of Education and the director of the State Library. By the unification law of 1904, the Home Education Division was placed under the Department of Education and is now called the Division of Educational Extension.

In Connecticut, a Public Library Committee appointed by the State Board of Education was created in 1893. This Committee has advisory powers, and is authorized to give direct financial aid to libraries. In 1903 an appropriation was made for traveling libraries, and a library visitor was appointed.

In 1894 Vermont passed a law similar to that of Massachusetts, and in 1900 established a system of traveling libraries, and appointed a secretary to make personal visits to libraries.

It will be noticed that in the beginning all the New England states, except New York, followed Massachusetts as a model and confined their work to giving direct financial aid to libraries, the features of traveling libraries and library visiting being added later.

The Wisconsin Commission was organized in 1895, and became the pioneer and model for work in the West. Its activities now include the department of library extension and visitation, the traveling library department, the library school opened in 1906, and the legislative reference library.

In Ohio, a Commission was established in 1896, to have charge of the State Library and appoint the state librarian. Traveling libraries are operated as a department of the State Library. In 1906 an amendment to the law authorized the appointment of a library organizer, who began work in the fall of 1908, when the appropriation became available.

The Georgia Commission, established in 1897, is advisory only and has had no appropriation.

In 1899, commissions were established in seven states, two more following in 1900, and five others in 1901. Of these states, the group in the Middle West—Indiana, Iowa, Minnesota and Nebraska—followed the lines laid down by Wisconsin, each having a system of traveling libraries, and emphasizing field work and instruction. Since the conditions and problems of the states in the Middle West were found to be similar, it was believed that coöperation in publication of necessary printed matter would be an economy. At a conference of the library commissions of Wisconsin, Iowa and Minnesota, in October, 1901, plans for coöperative work were discussed, and as a result, Wisconsin contributed the *Suggestive list of books for a small library,* with supplementary *Buying-lists of recent books;* Minnesota edited and published the *Handbook of library organization;* and the *Quarterly* published by Iowa was for a time utilized by the other states, but after a few issues this plan proved to be impracticable. Of the Western states which established commissions at this time, Idaho and Kansas confined their efforts to traveling libraries, while the Colorado Commission, with no regular appropriation, has been an advisory body only.

Michigan aids in the organization and extension of libraries through two agencies: the State Library has charge of the traveling library system, and supplies books to communities having no libraries; the Board of Library Commissioners are concerned with building up town libraries, and to this end have a system of registered free libraries to which 100 books are loaned for six months. Each library in the state, through a mandatory law, must make a report to its county commissioner of schools, who in turn must make a report of every district, school and public library in his county to the Board of Library Commissioners.

Pennsylvania, which established its Commission in 1899, has a system of traveling libraries sent out under the direction of the state librarian. In 1907, a consulting librarian was appointed to further the extension work. Of the Eastern group of states, Maine, New Jersey and Delaware followed the plan of their neighboring states in offering direct financial aid to public libraries, all of them adding the feature of traveling libraries. Maine held a summer school in 1904, and again in 1910. Delaware employed an organizer for a time, and New Jersey has employed an organizer since 1905, and conducts a summer school.

In Maryland the State Library Commission encourages the establishment of libraries, and operates a system of traveling libraries. An organizer is sent out for a few months service when funds are available.

In Washington, a Commission was established in 1901, but in 1903 the law was changed, giving the Commission charge of the State Library. By the law of 1907, the traveling library work was placed in the hands of a superintendent of traveling libraries, appointed by the Commission, but independent of the State Library.

In 1903, California established an Extension Department of the State Library to carry on the various branches of commission work.

The Colorado Traveling Library Commission was created in 1903, and conducts a system of traveling libraries.

Oregon joined the list in 1905, the law establishing this Commission being in some respects more comprehensive than any heretofore adopted, in that control of school libraries is vested in the Commission. The Commission prepares the list of books for school libraries from which selections must be made for purchases from the county library fund. The Legislature of 1907 amended the Commission law in three particulars—striking out the limit on the printing, omitting the section which apportions the funds, and increasing the appropriation from $2,000 to $6,000 a year.

No new commissions were created in 1906, but Virginia made provision for enlargement of the work of the State Library, and inaugurated a system of traveling libraries under the direction of the State Library Board.

In 1907, library commissions were established in Missouri and North Dakota. In Missouri, the law authorizes supervision of school libraries and courses of lectures on library administration in the Normal Schools in addition to the usual lines of commission work. In North Dakota the first work of the Commission was the reorganization of the system of traveling libraries formerly under the Department of Public Instruction, and the establishment of a legislative reference department. In the same year Alabama joined the ranks of states providing support for library work and enterprise, when a law was passed adding to the work of the Department of Archives and History, the duties usually performed by state library commissions, and providing for legislative reference work.

In 1909, legislation authorizing library extension work was enacted in Illinois, North Carolina, Tennessee, Texas and Utah, while in North Dakota the appropriation was increased from $1,500 to $7,800 annually, and the law was amended to give a commission of five members instead of three, as formerly, and longer tenure of offiee.

In Illinois, an amendment to the library law authorized the commissioners of the State Library to appoint two persons, who, together with the state librarian shall constitute the Illinois Library Extension Commission. The Commission is authorized to appoint a library organizer to carry on the usual lines of extension work, and to operate a system of traveling libraries. The appropriation for the work is $1,500 a year.

In North Carolina, a Library Commission of five members was created with the usual advisory powers, and authorized to operate a system of traveling libraries. Its annual appropriation is $1,500.

The Tennessee Free Library Commission was established by a similar law, with no appropriation.

The Texas Library and Historical Commission was established to control and administer the State Library, in which a legislative reference section is to be maintained, and to aid and encourage public libraries, but without the necessary funds to carry on extension work.

In Utah, a promoting commission appointed by the Superintendent of Public Instruction in 1907 carried on a successful campaign of library education, and in 1909, a Library-Gymnasium Commission of five members, was established by the Legislature to be appointed by the State Board of Education, and to be under its general supervision. Its purpose is to encourage the establishment of free libraries and gymnasiums, and its appropriation is $2,000.

The Kentucky Library Commission was established in 1910, with an appropriation of $6,000 a year. The law authorizes the usual methods of commission work, including a system of traveling libraries, and also provides that the secretary shall be a person trained in modern library methods. For fuller accounts of the growth and development of library extension work through state agency, see the publications of the various commissions as listed under each commission, as well as the following:

Public Libraries, February 1905.

(A Library Commission number containing State aid to libraries, by Gratia A. Countryman; Instructional work of library commissions, by Alice S. Tyler; Reports of Commissions; Value and work of a state library organizer, by W. R. Eastman. Synopsis of laws authorizing library commissions, by Johnson Brigham. This number was the first attempt to collect in one place data regarding the various commissions, and became the basis for the Year-book of the League.)

Brigham .... Model library commission law. Lib. J. 30: C 46-50.

Countryman . Lines of work which a state commission can profitably undertake. Lib. J. 25: C 51-54.

Galbreath .... Coöperation of state librarians and state library commissions. Lib. J. 25: C 54-57.

Hewins ..... Work of an Eastern library commission. Lib. J. 30: C 51-55.

Langton ..... What a permanent library commission can do to aid libraries. Pub. Lib. 9: 212-16.

Legler .... State library commissions. Lib. J. 30: C 40-45.

Stearns ...... How to organize state library commissions and make state aid effective. Lib. J. 24: C 16-18.

Thomson .... How to secure a state library commission. Lib. J. 26: C 191.

Tyler .... Work of library extension in Iowa. Pub. Lib. 9: 296-99.

LEAGUE OF LIBRARY COMMISSIONS.

The success of the experiment in coöperation which was inaugurated in 1901 by the library commissions of Wisconsin, Minnesota and Iowa, led to the suggestion that a national organization might more economically carry forward coöperative work. Printed matter of common interest and value to these commissions could thus be issued jointly, leaving to the overcrowded state commission workers more time and money for the problems peculiar to each state.

A preliminary conference representing four library commissions of the Middle West was held in Chicago, August 12, 1904, to discuss the advisability of an organization of library commissions. A committee was appointed to prepare a suggestive plan as to organization and methods of coöperative work. At the meeting of the Commissions' Section of the A. L. A., October 21, 1904, during the St. Louis conference, the committee made a report based on the experiments in coöperation in the Middle West, and on the replies received from letters sent to the various commissions. It was the unanimous opinion of those present that a League of Library Commissions should be organized. This organization was therefore at once effected by the creation of an executive board composed of one member from each of the ten states represented at that meeting, as follows: Connecticut, Indiana, Iowa, Minnesota, Nebraska, New Jersey, New York, Pennsylvania, Virginia, Wisconsin.

The Board organized immediately by the election of Mr. Henry E. Legler, Wisconsin, as chairman, and Miss Alice S. Tyler, Iowa, as secretary. An executive committee was selected from the states represented to formulate a coöperative plan of work. This committee consisted of the chairman, secretary and four additional members, Miss Marvin, Wisconsin; Miss Hoagland, Indiana; Miss Bullock, Nebraska, and Miss Baldwin, Minnesota.

At a meeting of this committee in Chicago, November 28 and 29, plans were considered for the immediate preparation and issue of a new edition of the *Suggestive list of books for a small library* and for the continuation of the *Buying list of recent books,* as the most urgent needs of the commissions. The executive committee also prepared, in the form of resolutions, a suggested plan for coöperation with the A. L. A. Publishing Board in the issuance of some of its publications.

In January, 1905, the A. L. A. Publishing Board began the publication of the *A. L. A. Book-list,* and the Executive Board of the League assured the Publishing Board of its support in that undertaking by its adoption by the commissions for use in the respective states. The *Buying list* which had formerly been compiled by the Wisconsin Commission for the use of the commissions of the Middle West was therefore discontinued.

At this time no definite arrangements could be made with the Publishing Board for other publications, and accordingly the League proceeded with the publication of the *Suggestive list of books for a small library,* compiled by Miss Cornelia Marvin, then of the Wisconsin Commission, and the second edition of the pamphlet on *U. S. Government documents in small libraries,* by J. I. Wyer, Jr.

During the Portland meeting of the A. L. A., a conference was held between representatives of the Publishing Board and the Executive Board of the League to discuss methods of coöperation. The needs of the commissions for certain printed matter were fully conceded by the members of the Publishing Board and it was recognized that in supplying these the Board would be complying with the condition of Mr. Carnegie's gift of $100,000 to the A. L. A., "the income of which should be applied to the preparation and publication of such reading lists, indexes, and other bibliographical and library aids as would be specially useful in the circulating libraries of the country." At the regular meeting of the Publishing Board held in October, 1905, it was agreed that the Board would publish any material furnished by the League.

At the meeting of the Commissions section of the A. L.
A. at Portland the organization of the League was approved
by that section, and it was unanimously voted with the approval of the A. L. A. Council, that the League of Library Commissions as affiliated with the A. L. A. be sub-
stituted for the Library Commissions section.

A meeting of the Executive Board was held in Indianapolis, Dec. 13-14, 1905, when final consideration was given
to the constitution and by-laws of the League and the subject of the publications of the League and A. L. A. Publishing Board was fully discussed.

Regular annual meetings of the League since its organization as an affiliated body with the A. L. A. have been
held each year in conjunction with the A. L. A. conference.
The mid-winter meeting of the Executive Board, held in
Chicago about the first of January each year, has developed
into an informal conference of commission workers and
others interested in extension work, for a discussion of commission problems. Mid-winter conferences of library commissions of the Eastern states were held in Hartford,
Conn., in 1909, and 1910, and in Albany, N. Y. in 1910.

Twenty-six states are now members of the League, in-
cluding Alabama, California, Connecticut, Delaware, Georgia,
Illinois, Indiana, Iowa, Kentucky, Massachusetts, Michigan,
Minnesota, Missouri, Nebraska, New Jersey, New York,
North Carolina, North Dakota, Ohio, Oregon, Pennsylvania,
Rhode Island, Tennessee, Vermont, Washington and Wiscon-
sin.

For further information regarding the history and work
of the League, see:
Affiliation with A. L. A. Lib. J. 30: C 192-94. Pub. Lib.
          10: 415.
Tyler. League of Library Commissions. Lib. J. 30: 274-77.
Annual meeting, Narragansett, 1906. Lib. J. 31: C 282-84.
———— Asheville, 1907. A. L. A. Bulletin. 1: 231-45. Lib. J.
          32: 318-21. Pub. Lib. 12: 279.
———— Lake Minnetonka, 1908. A. L. A. Bulletin. 2: 305-
          17. Lib. J. 33: 277-79. Pub. Lib. 13: 276-80.

—— Bretton Woods, 1909. A. L. A. Bulletin. **3**: 337-355. Lib. J. **34**: 359-362. Pub. Lib. **14**: 313.

—— Mackinac Island, 1910. A. L. A. Bulletin. **4** (Proceedings number) Lib. J. **35**: 317-318. Pub. Lib. **15**: 352.

Midwinter meeting, Indianapolis, December 1905. Lib. J. **31**: 27.

—— Chicago, January, 1907. Lib. J. **32**: 76-77. Pub. Lib. **12**: 67.

—— Chicago, January, 1908. Lib. J. **33**: 59-62. Pub. Lib. **13**: 49-53.

—— Chicago, January, 1909. Lib. J. **34**: 63-64. Pub. Lib. **14**: 65-66.

—— Chicago, January, 1910. Lib. J. **35**: 69. Pub. Lib. **15**: 72-74.

—— Hartford, February, 1909, Pub. Lib. **14**: 150.

—— Hartford, January, 1910. Lib. J. **35**: 122.

—— Albany, February, 1910. Lib. J. **35**: 28. Pub. Lib. **15**: 132.

PUBLICATIONS.

(Arranged chronologically)

U. S. Government documents in small libraries; by **J. I.** Wyer, Jr., Ed. 2. May, 1905. (o. p.)
(New ed. issued by A. L. A. Publishing Board, 1910)

Suggestive list of books for a small library; compiled by Cornelia Marvin. Part 1, Adults. June, 1905. (o. p.)

Year-book of library commissions; compiled by Clara **F.** Baldwin, May, 1906. (o. p.)

—— May, 1907. (o. p.)

—— December, 1908. (o. p.)

Magazines for the small library; by Katharine MacDonald Jones, 1908. (o. p.)

—— New ed. 1909. Paper, 10 cents.

Anniversaries and holidays; ed. by Mary Emogene Hazeltine, April, 1909. Paper, 25 cents.

Report of committee on essentials of a model commission law, 1909. Free.

Report of committee on commission work in state institutions, 1909. Free.

Handbook of library commissions; compiled by Clara F. Baldwin, December, 1910. Paper, 25 cents.

Publications Reprinted by the League.

Report on standards of library training, by A. L. A. Committee, 1905. (o. p.)

The organization of a library in a small town, by Elizabeth D. Renninger, 1906. (o. p.)

How shall a small town make a library beginning? by Alice S. Tyler, 1906. (o. p.)

Buffalo Public Library Graded list of books for schools. 1909. (League ed. o. p.)

Buying list of books for small libraries; compiled by Zaidee Brown. 1910. (League ed. o. p.)

Graded list of stories for reading aloud; compiled by Harriot E. Hassler. New ed. 1910. Paper, 10 cents.

Publications Issued for the League by the A. L. A. Publishing Board.

Small library buildings, compiled by Cornelia Marvin, $1.25.

Foreign Book Lists;—German, 50c. Norwegian and Danish, 25c. Swedish, 25c.

Library Tract No. 10. Why do we need a public library? Material for a library campaign, by Chalmers Hadley. 5c.

Library Handbooks. 15c each.

3 Management of traveling libraries, by Edna D. Bullock.

6 Mending and repair of books, by Margaret W. Brown.

7 U. S. Government documents in small libraries, by J. I. Wyer, Jr.

LEAGUE OF LIBRARY COMMISSIONS.
CONSTITUTION.

Name. The name of this organization shall be League of Library Commissions.

2

Object. The object of the League shall be to promote, by coöperation, such library interests as are within the province of library supervision by the state.

3

Membership. Any state commission, board, bureau, department, or other official organization charged with the duty of promoting library interests in the state where it is located, either by means of traveling libraries or the establishment, organization and supervision of public libraries, shall be eligible to membership upon compliance with the conditions hereinafter enumerated.

Each organization admitted to active membership shall have one vote through an accredited representative (preferably an executive officer) on any subject requiring action at any meeting; but any member or officer of such commission, board or department may attend the meetings of the League and share in its deliberations.

4

Officers. The officers of the League shall be president, 1st and 2nd vice-presidents, and secretary-treasurer, who shall be elected at the annual meeting and shall serve until election of their successors.

5

Executive Board. Except when the League is in session, its affairs shall be in the hands of an Executive Board consisting of the officers named in Section 4 and the members of the Publication Committee, as hereinafter provided. Any vacancy occurring during the year shall be filled by the remaining members of the Executive Board.

The Executive Board shall arrange for the printing of such publications as may be found most useful in commission wôrk, and shall fix the price at which material published by the League may be sold.

Votes of the Executive Board may be taken by correspondence, a majority vote being necessary to give validity to any action so taken.

The Executive Board of the League shall prepare programs, select topics and assign speakers for the annual meeting and make all the necessary arrangements therefor.

6

Committees. There shall be a Publication Committee of three members who shall secure suitable material required in printed form for field work and in the organization and equipment of libraries.

Standing committees and special committees not otherwise provided for shall be appointed by the president.

7

Dues. The payment of a yearly membership fee of five dollars ($5.00) shall constitute active membership, such members being entitled to secure League publications at cost and to exercise the voting privilege as specified in Section 3. Associate members paying no dues shall be charged regular price for League publications but may participate in deliberations without a vote.

8

Annual Meeting. The annual meeting of the League shall be held at the time and place of the annual meeting of the A. L. A.

9

Affiliation. The League shall be affiliated with the A. L. A. in accordance with its constitution and by-laws.

10

By-Laws. The Board may adopt by-laws for the League subject to such amendment as may be voted at the annual meeting.

11

Amendments. Amendments to this constitution may be adopted at any annual meeting of the League by a two-thirds vote of those present entitled to vote; provided that notice shall have been given, by correspondence, to all members of the League at least two months prior to such annual meeting; or in lieu thereof, that the amendment shall have received the unanimous approval of the Executive Board.

ORGANIZATION AND ACTIVITIES OF COMMISSIONS.

ALABAMA

The work of public and school library extension, and allied activities, such as are usually performed by library commissions, is carried on under the direction of a Library Extension Division of the State Department of Archives and History, with headquarters in the State Capitol, Montgomery, authorized by act approved March 5, 1907, and put in operation June 1, 1907.

Library Legislation.   Library legislation in Alabama is quite limited, and yet it is sufficiently comprehensive to meet the needs of practically unlimited expansion, with the single exception of appropriations for direct aid. These laws may be grouped as (1) the statutory provisions for the organization and support of a State and Supreme Court Library; (2) the maintenance of historical and legislative reference collections by the Department of Archives and History; (3) a very few special acts incorporating local library associations; (4) provision for unlimited municipal support; (5) the legislation for the organization of the Library Extension Division. The following is the very comprehensive and elastic provision requiring the organization of this Division:

·"It shall encourage and assist in the establishment of public and school libraries, and in the improvement and strengthening of those already in existence; it shall give advice and provide assistance to libraries and library workers in library administration, methods and economy; and it shall conduct a system of traveling libraries."

Advisory and Promotion Work. The efforts of the Division, from its very beginning, have been directed to arousing and shaping public opinion throughout the state looking to the establishment of new public and school libraries, as well as to the strengthening of those already in existence. This has been done through correspondence, public addresses, and personal visits and advice on the part of the Director and the assistant in charge of the Library Extension Division. The Division responds to all reasonable calls for assistance in the matter of advice and help in developing interest. The press, the club women, and heads of educational institutions have been valuable allies in the movement. There has always been a very close affiliation between the Alabama Library Association and the Library Extension Division of the state. The office of the extension division is headquarters of the Association and the work of each is coöperative with that of the other.

Instruction. Beginning in 1908, the Division has conducted a five weeks summer course in library training, which will be offered each year.

Through correspondence, advice, in so far as it is possible, is given on all subjects of library administration, methods and economy to Alabama librarians and library workers.

Traveling Libraries. The first traveling library went out Nov. 4, 1907. Stations have been established mainly in rural communities and schools. During 1910, the Division acquired by gift about one hundred books printed in type for the blind. This forms the nucleus of a collection for circulation among the blind readers of the state.

Publications:

Laws governing the Department of Archives and History, 1907.

Library Extension Circular.

Executive Staff:

Thomas M. Owen, Director, Alabama State Department of Archives and History, Montgomery.

Miss Tommie Dora Barker, Library Extension Assistant, Montgomery.

CALIFORNIA

The California State Library carries on the work which in many states is under the supervision of a public library commission. Formerly the headquarters of the extension work was the Extension Department, but now every department of the library is active along extension lines. The counties, too, are coöperating in the work since the county library law was passed and ten counties are already doing some of the work for their territory that was at first handled from the State Library. The changes are made in an attempt to develope the most economical system possible for the existing conditions in California.

Branches of the State Library. An act passed by the Legislature of 1909 makes it possible for the State Library to establish branches and as soon as the State Library fund allows they will be established in San Francisco and Los Angeles.

Organizing. Library organizers are employed to investigate library conditions, to encourage the establishment of libraries, to visit those already established, to give advice and assistance to libraries throughout the state, to consult with trustees and architects regarding library buildings and to explain to the people generally the plan for the library development in California. This assistance is all given free by the State Library.

Instruction. The State Library held an institute at the annual meeting of the California Library Association held in San José in 1908 and also at the annual meeting in

Long Beach in April, 1910. In this way something has been done toward helping those librarians who have problems unsolved. The head of the Catalog Department of the State Library was the head instructor at the institute in 1910.

The State Library and all others interested will make every effort to have some sort of library school established as soon as possible.

Traveling Libraries. From the Traveling Libraries Division of the Extension Department, fixed groups of 50 volumes each are loaned to any community without a public library, on application of five resident tax payers. There is no charge for the use of the libraries and transportation both ways is paid by the State Library. A library may be kept three months, and by special permission the time may be extended three months longer.

These libraries have either created a demand for books in remote communities and other communities without libraries, or they have proved without doubt that the demand exists. So that very soon a very much more economical way of supplying this sort of books and of meeting the rapidly growing demand for more books will be worked out for the state. The county free library system as tried for the last two years in Sacramento county and a shorter time in eight other counties, shows already that it will solve this problem most satisfactorily.

Clubs and Granges. Collections of books for study purposes are sent to any club or grange upon application of two resident taxpayers. As these books are selected from the main collection of the State Library, the work is carried on entirely by the Reference Department. No fee is charged and transportation both ways is paid by the State Library. Books may be kept three months, and by special permission the time may be extended.

The reference librarian is sent to meetings of clubs and granges to explain what those organizations can get from the State Library.

Legislative Reference Department. The legislative reference work is carried on by the legislative and municipal reference department of the library. This department also coöperates with the Reference Department in furnishing material to the high schools and clubs for their debates.

Books for the Blind. Embossed books in any type requested, samples of appliances, games, etc., are sent to any blind resident of the state—and many outside the state—upon application to the Books for the Blind Division of the Extension Department. Books for the blind are also loaned to free public libraries or reading rooms, in collections of from ten to twenty-five books, upon application from the trustees of such library or reading room, if there will be at least five borrowers to make use of them. The books may be kept two months, and the transportation is paid both ways .by the State Library.

School Libraries. The State Library has not undertaken to assist the school libraries. Those interested believe that the county library system with a branch or deposit station in each school will most successfully solve the question of school libraries in this state.

Publications:
  Libraries of California, 1904.
  News notes of California libraries, May, 1906- date.
  The California State Library is yours.
  County library system for California.
  Extension Department.
  Circular no. 1 Rules for lending traveling libraries.
  Finding lists 1-47.
  —— Books for the Blind Division.
  Circular and finding list. 3d ed.
  ——Public Libraries Division.
  Circular no. 1 Why a town should incorporate.

Law Department.
Library laws of California, 1909.
Legislative and Municipal Reference Department.
Legislative reference bulletin no. 1 Hints for drawing
  legislative bills.
——no. 2 River improvement laws in other states and
  countries.

Board of Trustees:
W. C. Van Fleet, President, San Francisco.
Allen B. Lemmon, Santa Rosa.
Bradner W. Lee, Los Angeles.
R. M. Richardson, Sacramento.
Charles S. Greene, Oakland.

Library Staff:
James L. Gillis, State Librarian, Sacramento.
Milton J. Ferguson, Assistant Librarian.
Miss Laura Steffens, 2d Asst. Librarian, in charge of Ex-
  tension Department.
Miss Mabel R. Gillis, 1st Asst. in Extension Department.
Miss Elizabeth C. Haines, Assistant.
Miss Mary V. Provines, Assistant.
Miss Bertha Kumli, Library Organizer.
Miss Harriet G. Eddy, County Library Organizer.

COLORADO

The Board of Library Commissioners gives advice upon
library matters through the Denver Public Library and the
publication of the library laws of the state has led to the establishment of libraries in a number of towns.

The Board has had no regular appropriation, and has
no employees.

Publications:
Colorado library laws.
Colorado state documents check list. (In preparation.)

Members of the Commission:
Charles R. Dudley, President, Public Library, Denver.
George M. Lee, Secretary, Denver.
Edwin H. Park.
Harper Leiper.
Alfred E. Whitaker, Boulder.

The Colorado Traveling Libraries' Commission was established in 1903, through the efforts of the Colorado Federation of Women's Clubs, for the purpose of maintaining and developing the system of traveling libraries which had been inaugurated by the Federation in 1899.

The law provides that all members of the Commission shall be women, appointed by the governor from a list submitted by the Executive board of the Federation.

Traveling Libraries are loaned without charge to any town in the state upon application, the person to whom the box is sent being personally responsible for their safe return at the end of six months.

The libraries are of three kinds: (1) Miscellaneous collections of 50 volumes each, intended for the use of the general public; (2) Juvenile libraries of 50 volumes each, for use in country schools, Sunday schools and the industrial schools, and (3) Small collections of reference books for the use of clubs and study classes.

The Commission distributes boxes of magazines and paper bound books to farmers, mill-men, railroad-men, hospitals, engine houses, stations, jails, reformatories and prisons. These are not returned but are used and passed on until worn out. Through the coöperation of the club women in the different towns throughout the state the work of establishing a chain of library stations for the distribution of periodicals has been undertaken. Leaflets for the sick, which are short stories taken from magazines and mounted, are sent to hospitals, relief corps, aid societies and branches of the Sunshine Society.

Publications:
Biennial reports, 1906- date.

Members of the Commission:
Mrs. Julia V. Welles, President, Denver.
————, Vice-President.
Mrs. James D. Whitmore, Secretary, Denver.
Mrs. B. F. Stickley, Historian, Leadville.
Mrs. Z. X. Snyder, Reader, Greeley.

Executive Officer:
Miss Carrie M. Cushing, Transportation Clerk, Capitol Building, Denver.

CONNECTICUT

The Free Public Library Committee revises book-lists sent by towns, and spends the state grant to the best of its ability, gives advice and assistance to librarians and teachers, tries to establish new libraries and make subscription libraries free, holds neighborhood meetings, publishes documents and book-lists, and circulates traveling libraries, bird charts and pictures, framed and unframed.

Advisory Work. The first work of the Public Library Committee of Connecticut was to issue circulars of information explaining the library law and its provision for state aid to public libraries. Members of the Committee have visited many towns to make addresses on the advantages of the library. In 1903, an official visitor and inspector of libraries was appointed, who visits the libraries to confer with the librarian, to offer suggestions for improvement, and to report to the Committee on conditions. The Committee also issues lists of books, other documents, and revises the book-lists sent by the towns applying for state aid.

Instruction. Institutes, or neighborhood meetings, as they are called, are held at irregular intervals, at points where

· there seems to be special need or opportunity. These include eight or ten towns, and lessons in mending and repairing and simple talks on cataloging, classification, the use of pictures, work with children, etc., are given. Suggestions for small libraries have been published.

Organizing. At the expense of the Public Library Committee, the visitor and inspector spends as much time as is possible with small libraries in directing the cataloging. Sometimes a cataloger is sent to assist in the work.

Direct Aid. If the town appropriates $200 or less for the establishment of a public library, the state will give an equal amount in books. If a town appropriates $100 or less annually for the maintenance of a public library, the state will give an equal amount in books. The lists of books sent in by the town are revised and approved by the committee, before the grant is allowed.

Traveling Libraries. The traveling libraries consist of libraries of a general character, circulated among neighborhoods and public libraries; libraries for school use, circulated among schools; libraries on special subjects, accompanied by pictures, loaned to clubs and libraries; libraries in foreign languages, circulated among neighborhoods and libraries, and home libraries loaned to individuals and families. In addition to the collections owned by the Committee, libraries loaned by the Connecticut Society of Colonial Dames, the Connecticut Audubon Society and by women's clubs and individuals are circulated among neighborhoods and schools.

The Committee also has a large collection of miscellaneous pictures, framed and unframed, a part owned by the Committee, and a part loaned by the Connecticut Society of Colonial Dames, which are circulated among schools and libraries.

School Libraries. School libraries in Connecticut have a grant from the state and are permitted to buy books through the Public Library Committee.

The Society of Colonial Dames circulates through the

Committee, traveling libraries and portfolios of pictures to schools. The libraries are sent to schools, express paid, and may be retained three months. The books are sent in a box which may be used as a book-case in the school room. As a condition of this loan, the teacher is required to keep a record of circulation.

The Audubon Society sends out libraries, portfolios and sets of bird-charts to schools.

Publications:

Reports, 1893-1894, 1897-1900.
> (Reports for other years are included in the reports of the State Board of Education.)

Annual lists of books, 1897-1903.

Monthly book-list, 1904-1907.

What a free library does for a country town, 1894.

Circular relating to public libraries, 1894-1897.

Method of obtaining state grant to public libraries, 1902, 1904.

Traveling school libraries loaned by Colonial Dames, 1902, 1904, 1909.

Pictures loaned to schools by Colonial Dames, 1902, 1903.

Books on the Far East, 1904.

Address at the reopening of the Acton Library, Old Saybrook, June, 30, 1904, by Rev. Samuel Hart, D. D.

The development of public libraries within the bounds of the old New Haven Colony, 1904.

The public library and its critics, 1906.

List of public library directors, 1906.

A selected list of literature relating to American forests and forestry, 1906.

List of pictures, framed and unframed, to be loaned to schools and libraries, 1906.

Grange traveling libraries, series B and series C.

Helps in library work with children, 1909.

Novels and children's stories of 1908-9.

Thanksgiving references, 1909.

Address of Simeon E. Baldwin, at the laying of the corner-stone of the Connecticut state library, May 25, 1909.

Members of the Committee:

Charles D. Hine, Chairman, Hartford.

Miss Caroline M. Hewins, Secretary, Hartford.

H. A. Tirrell, Norwich.

Edwin B. Gager, Derby.

Storrs O. Seymour, Litchfield.

Executive Officer:

Mrs. Belle Holcomb Johnson, Visitor and Inspector of libraries, State House, Hartford.

DELAWARE

The State Library Commission was established in 1901, to promote the establishment and efficiency of free public libraries in incorporated towns. In 1903 the law regarding the establishment of public libraries was amended so that now it is possible for any school district in the state to establish a public library. The Commission has made an effort to have every incorporated town vote on the question of establishing a library under this law. Advice and assistance is given to towns in the establishment of libraries, and statistics of libraries are collected.

Direct Aid. An amount equal to one-half the minimum amount authorized to be raised in districts of its class may be given annually to each public library. This varies from $12.50 to $125.

Traveling Libraries. The commission maintains a system of traveling libraries which have been acquired by gift and by purchase.

Each library contains about 50 volumes, and is loaned for three months with privilege of renewal. They are sent free of charge to: (1) Any school, Sunday school, college or seminary upon application of its principal; (2) Any village, town or community, study or other club, grange, post, lodge, busi-

ness corporation or other similar organization, which will
form a library association of not less than five members; (3)
Any library upon application of its trustees or commissioners.

A few collections of books for study are loaned to women's
clubs and special loans are made to teachers, and also to individuals when possible to give assistance to those pursuing
special lines of study.

Publications:
Biennial reports, 1907-date.
Circular of information.
Handbook, 1904.

Members of the Commission:
Daniel W. Corbit, Odessa, Chairman.
Mrs. James W. Anthony, Smyrna.
A. L. Bailey, Wilmington.
I. J. Brasure, Selbyville.
Mrs. C. E. Burchenal, Wilmington.
H. P. Cannon, Bridgeville.
Mrs. Chas. E. Miller, Wilmington.
Mrs. Henry Ridgely, Dover.
A. M. Daly, Dover.

Executive Staff:
H. Ridgely Harrington, State Librarian, Secretary, Dover.
Miss Ida V. Culbreth, Librarian.

GEORGIA

The Georgia Library Commission was established in 1897,
to give advice and counsel to all communities in the state regarding the establishment and management of libraries. The
Commission may also send its members to aid in organizing
new libraries or improving those already established. The
Commission has had no appropriation since its organization,
but through the coöperation of the Carnegie Library of Atlanta has rendered much assistance to all library undertakings in
the South.

Publications:
Handbook of the libraries of the State of Georgia, Atlanta, 1907. (Printed as a special Bulletin of the Carnegie Library of Atlanta.)

Members of the Commission:
Miss Julia Rankin, Atlanta, Chairman.
Mrs. J. K. Ottley, Atlanta.
Walter Brooks, Rome.
Carleton B. Gibson, Columbus.
Bridges Smith, Macon.

Executive Officer:
Mrs. Percival Sneed, Organizer, Carnegie Library, Atlanta.

IDAHO

The State Library Commission operates a system of traveling libraries under the control of the Superintendent of Public Instruction, who is ex-officio secretary of the Commission.

The libraries consist of 50 books each and are loaned to any community in the state upon application of five tax-payers, remaining at each station four months. A competent person is appointed librarian and is made responsible for the books. The expense of transportation, which is a very large item in this state, is borne by the Commission.

Publications:
Handbook of Idaho Library Commission.
Biennial report, 1906-date.

Members of the Commission:
D. C. McDougall, Attorney General, Chairman, Boise.
James A. McLean, President of the University of Idaho, Moscow.
Miss S. Belle Chamberlain, Superintendent of Public Instruction, Boise.
Robert Lansdon, Secretary of State, Boise.

Executive Staff:
  Miss S. Belle Chamberlain, Secretary, ex-officio, Boise.
  Miss E. Louise Johnson, Assistant Secretary.

Illinois

The bill providing for the establishment of the Illinois Library Extension Commission was passed on June 14th, 1909 and became a law on July 1st, 1909. The members of the Commission provided for by the law were appointed in September, 1909, by the State Library Commission which is the governing body of the State Library. This Commission consists of the Governor, Secretary of State and Superintendent of Public Instruction. The Organizer was appointed in January, 1910, and assumed active duties March 1st, 1910.

Advisory Work. It is the duty of the Commission to give advice and information to the librarian or trustees of any existing public library, or to any person or community interested in starting a new public library, concerning the organization, maintenance or administration of any such. The Commission shall operate traveling libraries and through its organizer keep informed of the condition, scope and methods of work of the various public libraries of the state.

The advisory work of the Commission is done through the organizer by correspondence or personal visits wherever a desire for such is expressed. This is the largest part of the work at the present time as neither funds nor time permit of organizing libraries in the sense that is usually understood by that term. The name organizer in this Commission is equivalent to that of secretary in most of the Commissions.

Traveling Libraries. The Illinois Federation of Women's Clubs presented the Commission with its Traveling Library collections and the collections are being reorganized into one general collection. This was considered the best plan of procedure owing to the large percentage of fiction in the collections.

The only work now being done with school libraries is the temporary loan of a traveling library to supplement the school collection.

Publication:
    Leaflet No. 1. What the Illinois Library Extension Commission means to Illinois.

Members of the Commission:
    James A. Rose, Secretary of State, Chairman, Springfield.
    Mrs. Eugenie M. Bacon, Secretary, Decatur.
    Joseph H. Freeman, Aurora.

Executive Officer:
    Miss Eugenia Allin, Organizer, Decatur.*

Indiana

The Public Library Commission endeavors to secure the establishment of public libraries in localities able to support them, visits libraries for the purpose of giving advice and instruction, conducts a summer school for librarians, co-operates with the Indiana Library Association in holding district meetings, maintains a system of traveling libraries, and endeavors to bring about a closer relation between libraries and other educational agencies.

Advisory Work.   The secretary and state organizer gives much of his time to advisory work through correspondence and in personal visits to towns. Interest in library matters is aroused and information is given as to the organization of libraries, building plans and furnishings, selection of books, methods of advertising, and in library administration. Numerous editorials are written by the secretary for newspapers

*Note:—The headquarters have been in Decatur, Ill. since organization but it is now expected that permanent quarters will be established in Springfield, Ill. early in 1911.

over the state regarding libraries, their establishment and their management. Addresses are given at clubs and public meetings when library questions are discussed. The Commission publishes a quarterly bulletin and also distributes free of charge to Indiana libraries, the A. L. A. and other book-lists.

Instruction. In addition to individual instruction given in the Commission's office to visiting librarians, summer library schools have been conducted each year beginning in 1902. Only those are admitted who have had a four years' High School course or its equivalent, and who are filling library positions or are under definite written appointment to them. The course includes a study of technical methods in library work and consideration is given also to questions of the library's relations to the public, etc. The class usually numbers about twenty students. The school was formerly conducted at Winona Lake, but has been held at Earlham College, Richmond, since 1908. About ninety lectures are given, including a dozen or more by visiting librarians.

Organization. The Commission helps to organize city, town and township libraries and if the income of the library is small, the organizer spends a few days at a time in instructing the local librarians how to classify the library. No charge is made for such services. When a library is able to pay for a cataloger's services, the Commission recommends some one who can do the work efficiently.

Traveling Libraries. The traveling libraries' system in Indiana was inaugurated in 1899, and was at first administered from the State Library. In 1902 the books were transferred to the office of the Commission. The books are divided into three groups; the general libraries, made up of forty volumes of miscellaneous books; the subject libraries, consisting of from twelve to twenty volumes on a special topic; the open shelf collection from which books are lent as desired. The books are lent to clubs, schools, and libraries, and to any community upon application of five citizens. The transportation charges are paid by the borrowers. Collections of books may be retained three months and may usually be renewed for another period of three months if desired.

Special effort is being made to have the traveling libraries supplement the collections of the small public libraries. In some cases a hundred or more volumes are sent to a town library to enable it to supply the needs of the whole township.

Institutes and District Meetings. In 1903 the Commission began holding institutes in different parts of the state, but in 1905 they were discontinued because of lack of funds. Under the new administration in 1907 the institutes were begun again and have been continued up to the present time. At its last convention, the Indiana Library Association provided for district meetings to be held in all parts of the state. These district meetings are under the control of a committee of which the Secretary of the Commission is ex-officio a member, and the Commission is expected to have a representative at the regular meeting in every district each year. This plan will make the institutes unnecessary as the same sort of work will be done at the district meetings as was formerly done at the institutes.

Institutional Libraries. Indiana was one of the first states to give aid to institutional libraries through its Library Commission. Several years ago assistance was given to the library at the Indiana Boys' School, but small appropriations have prevented the development of definite work in this field. A charging system was put in the Indiana Reformatory library, which proved very successful. Considerable help has been given by the Commission to the two institutional libraries above mentioned, and to the one at the Indiana Girls' School.

Building Plans. In order to help communities secure economical, convenient library buildings, the Commission has a collection of photographs and floor plans of several hundred library buildings. They have proved of great value to library architects and library boards and a decided improvement has resulted in library construction in towns where the plans have been lent. In addition to plans of buildings, the Commission has a small collection of blue print drawings showing dimensions and construction of shelving, newspaper and periodical racks, etc. The Commission believes that the best furniture purchasable is the cheapest for library boards, but when there is not sufficient money available for this; good, inexpensive furniture has been made from the blue prints and used until the library's income permitted the purchase of the best library furniture in the market.

Documents. The Public Library Commission and State Library are authorized by law to distribute state documents to public libraries. Except in a few cases, however, the distribution is done by the State Library.

Publications in Print:
> Graded list of stories for reading aloud; compiled by Harriot E. Hassler. 1910.
> Important laws of Indiana relating to Public libraries and the Public Library Commission of Indiana. 1910.
> Library development and the Public Library Commission of Indiana. 1908.
> Library Occurrent, 1906—date.
> Revised finding list of traveling libraries. 1908.
> Study club finding list. 1907.
> Report, 1901-04, 1906-08.
> Graded list of books for schools in the traveling libraries.
> Sources for obtaining material for miscellaneous picture collection.
> List of pictures for children's rooms.
> Helps in the selection of children's books.
> List of picture books by good illustrators.
> List of illustrated books for boys and girls.

Members of the Commission:
> Jacob P. Dunn, Indianapolis, President.
> Mrs. Elizabeth C. Earl, Connersville.
> William W. Parsons, Terre Haute.

Executive Staff:

Carl H. Milam, Secretary and State Organizer, The Capitol, Indianapolis.

Miss Carrie E. Scott, Assistant State Organizer.

Miss Helen Davis, Librarian, Traveling Libraries.

Iowa

The Library Commission of the State of Iowa serves as a Board of Library Extension and a Bureau of Library Information by means of its various activities.

The Commission gives advice and counsel by personal visits and correspondence, to all free and other public libraries in the state and to communities which propose to establish them, conducts a summer school, maintains a system of traveling libraries and an exchange for periodicals.

Advisory Work.　The secretary of the Commission has, through correspondence and personal visits, become acquainted with library conditions in the state and encouragement is given to all cities and towns to take advantage of the law providing for a municipal tax for a library. The advisory work of the secretary has included counsel in preliminary efforts for the submission of the library question to vote; advice as to methods of organization, selection of books, and recommendation of competent organizers; conferences with trustees regarding plans for new library buildings; addresses to teachers' meetings, women's clubs, public meetings, etc., on library subjects; and correspondence on many subjects relating to library extension.

Instruction.　The Commission conducts a summer school for library training at the State University of Iowa, as a regular department of the University Summer School. Those only are admitted who are already in library work or definitely appointed to positions. The course covers a period of six weeks, and includes technical details of library work, with special emphasis on classification and cataloging. Library work with children has been an important feature of the school. A second year's course in cataloging is offered every two or three years to those who have completed the first year's work satisfactorily and to those who have had sufficient previous training or experience. During the year, the secretary makes personal visits of a few days' duration to instruct librarians as to methods and assist in organizing.

The *Iowa Library Quarterly,* a sixteen-page bulletin, is published for the benefit of trustees and librarians of the free public libraries of Iowa.

Organizing. The secretary of the Commission gives as much time as possible to organizing town libraries and in the preliminary work, selection of books, etc. Where the income of the library is small the Commission gives the services of a skilled organizer in putting the library on a modern basis. If local funds are available libraries are expected to pay for the services of an organizer, the Commission aiding by advice and counsel and securing a capable worker.

Traveling Libraries. The Iowa Library Commission maintains a traveling library system as an important feature of its work.

The books may be loaned to a local public library, to a library association created for the purpose, to a group of ten taxpayers, to clubs, schools and other organizations, and to individuals, free of cost, except transportation. Regular libraries are loaned for three months, but an extension of time is allowed, when desired.

Two distinct collections of books are kept for traveling library purposes: the regular libraries arranged in fixed groups of 50 volumes each, consisting of miscellaneous collections for general reading; and the general loan, or "open shelf" collection, arranged by subject according to the Decimal classification, from which libraries are made up to meet the needs of the applicants. This collection includes (1) books for study clubs and other organizations, for which a selection of books best adapted to their requirements, and usually not exceeding 25 volumes, is made; (2) libraries for young people; (3) individual loans, which may be secured by filing an agreement guaranteed by the local bank, and (4) books for the blind, which are loaned to any blind person in the state, upon recommendation of a resident taxpayer acquainted with the applicant, or which may be loaned through the local library.

Documents. The Commission has prepared and published a Check-list of the Publications of the State of Iowa, as the first necessary step in regulating the distribution of state publications.

School Libraries. Traveling libraries are loaned to rural schools, books for this purpose being selected from a graded list issued by the State Board of Educational Examiners. Instruction is given in the Summer Library School to teachers on the care and use of school libraries.

Periodical Exchange. It has been found of great practical service to aid small libraries in completing sets of standard periodicals indexed in Poole; magazines are generously contributed from all parts of the state and there is no cost further than the payment of freight.

Publications in Print:
Iowa Library Quarterly; 1901 to date.
Leaflets:
No. 1. Shall a free public library be established?
No. 2. Iowa day and a few books about Iowa.
No. 3. Periodicals; their value and use.
No. 4. Birthdays, anniversaries and events.
No. 5. Free Traveling Library of Iowa.
No. 6. Books for the blind.
No. 7. Library buildings.
No. 8. Study club programs.
No. 9. Traveling picture collections.
No. 10. Making a library beginning.

List of books recommended for children's library; compiled by Annie Carroll Moore.

Traveling Library lists.

Check-list of state publications.

List of books by Iowa authors.

Reports, 1903, 1905, 1906, 1908.

Members of the Commission:

Johnson Brigham, State Librarian, Chairman, Des Moines.

George E. MacLean, President State University, Iowa City.

John F. Riggs, State Supt. of Public Instruction, Des Moines.

Mrs. Horace M. Towner, Corning.

Mrs. David W. Norris, Grinnell.

Mrs. Henry J. Howe, Marshalltown.

Captain W. H. Johnston, Ft. Dodge.

Executive Staff:

Miss Alice S. Tyler, Secretary and Director of Library Extension, State Historical Bldg., Des Moines.

Miss Margaret W. Brown, Librarian Traveling Library.

Miss Eliza E. Townsend, Field and Reference Assistant.

Miss Ida L. Lange, Organizer.

Miss Edna Lyman, Advisory Children's Librarian (Part time only).

KANSAS

The Traveling Libraries Commission maintains a system of traveling libraries, which are loaned to any community in the state upon application and payment of a fee of $2.00 to cover transportation charges. The libraries are made up to suit the individual, club, school or society ordering. The only fixed libraries are those planned and prepared for club and class work.

Publications:
Reports, 1900-date.

Members of the Commission:
James L. King, State Librarian, Chairman.
Lucy B. Johnston.
Mrs. Eustace Brown.
Julia E. Brown.
H. G. Larimer.

Executive Officer:
Mrs. Adrian Greene, Secretary, Topeka.

KENTUCKY

The Kentucky Library Commission came into existence by act of the legislature of 1910. This act provides for the appointment of five members by the governor, and an appropriation for its maintenance and support.

The purpose of the Commission is to promote the library interests of the state by increasing the usefulness of libraries already in existence, by the establishment of new ones in communities where none exist, and by the maintenance and operation of a widely circulating traveling library system reaching all parts of the state where needed.

Advisory Work. To promote the best efficiency of library work in the state the Library Commission will assist communities wishing to establish libraries by giving advice and assistance in arousing public interest, in securing a maintenance tax, and in the selection of suitable building plans and furniture. Estimates for equipment and specifications for furniture and shelving will be supplied and material, in the form of photographs and blue prints, illustrating these things will be collected and kept in the commission office for the use of library boards. Help will also be given in the organization and administration of the library and where possible an organizer will be sent to aid in this work.

To libraries already established the Commission will give advice and help in book selection and purchase, with suggestions for securing the best book lists, will aid in reference work and in all the details of library equipment and management. The Commission will also assist library boards in securing the services of competent librarians, when requested so to do.

Traveling Libraries. The traveling libraries which have for a number of years been maintained by the women's clubs in the mountains of Kentucky will be thoroughly reorganized and turned over to the Commission, and new libraries will be added by purchase.

These traveling libraries will consist of fixed groups of fifty or more well selected books for general reading and study for adults, young people and children. They will be sent free of charge, except the cost of transportation, and under such conditions and rules as shall protect the interests of the state and best increase the efficiency of the service.

In addition to the fixed groups of traveling libraries described above, an open shelf or subject collection will be a feature of the commission work, from which books may be borrowed to suit the special needs of study clubs, debating societies, farmers' clubs and individuals.

Publications:
  Circular of information No. 1.
  Kentucky Library Commission law.

Members of the Commission:
  *Miss Fannie C. Rawson, Chairman, Louisville.
  Miss May Stone, Hindman.
  Frank K. Kavanaugh, Frankfort.
  Mrs. George Alexander Flournoy, Paducah.
  William B. Doherty, Louisville.

---

*Miss Rawson has been elected secretary, her election to take effect when she shall have secured the training in modern library methods required by the library law. At that time another member will be appointed to fill her unexpired term on the Commission.

Executive Officer:
Miss Julia A. Robinson, Acting Secretary, The Capitol, Frankfort.

MAINE

The State Library Commission of Maine was established in 1899 "to encourage the establishment of free public libraries, to select the books to be purchased for traveling libraries and to advise the state librarian in reference thereto."

The law creating the Commission also authorized the loaning of books from the State Library, and established the system of traveling libraries.

Advisory Work.   The members of the Commission have attended the dedication of new libraries, and have given help and advice to such libraries when called upon.   In 1906 the Commission rendered assistance to the State Library Association by paying the expenses of two outside speakers at the annual meeting.

Instruction.   In 1904 and again in 1910, a summer class of three weeks in library training was held at the University of Maine.   The course of study included simple cataloging, classification, accessioning, shelf-listing, book-selection, ordering and reference work, with lectures upon various other subjects of interest such as rebinding, administration, assistants, reports, statistics, etc.

Direct Aid. Each public library upon its establishment is entitled to $100 worth of books and annually thereafter to an amount equal to 10 per cent of the amount appropriated and expended for the library.

Traveling Libraries.   Libraries of 50 volumes each are loaned to any free library in the state upon application of the librarian; or to any association composed of five or more persons residing in a town destitute of a free library. The fee is $2.50.   Books and documents from the State

Library may also be loaned to any responsible citizen of the state, on written application therefor and on payment of all express and carriage charges.

Publications:
Reports 1-3, 1900-1903.

Members of the Commission:

H. C. Prince, State Librarian, Secretary Ex-officio, Augusta.

Mrs. Kate C. Estabrooke, President, Orono.

W. H. Hartshorn, Lewiston.

Mrs. Lizzie Jewett-Butler, Mechanic Falls.

J. H. Winchester, Corinna.

MARYLAND

The State Library Commission was established to give advice and counsel to all free libraries and public school libraries in the state and to all communities proposing to establish them, and to maintain a system of traveling libraries.

Advisory Work. When funds have permitted, a field secretary and organizer has been employed to visit traveling library stations, to arouse interest in library matters and to obtain information regarding library needs in various parts of the state. Statistics of libraries in Maryland have been collected and published in the annual reports of the Commission.

Traveling Libraries. The Commission owns 91 traveling libraries, these cases being shipped from the Enoch Pratt Free Library, Baltimore. Libraries of about 35 volumes each are loaned for four months to any community upon application of at least three responsible citizens, and payment of a fee of 50 cents.

Books for the blind are sent from the Enoch Pratt Free Library to any blind person in the state, the Commission agreeing to hold itself responsible for the safe-keeping of the books, and to pay a small sum to the library to cover wear and tear.

Publications:
Reports, 1903-date.

Members of the Commission:
M. Bates Stephens, Superintendent of Public Instruction, President, Denton.
Bernard C. Steiner, Librarian, Enoch Pratt Free Library, Secretary, Baltimore.
Miss Lynn M. Shaffer, State Librarian, Annapolis.
Mrs. John M. Carter, Mt. Washington.
Mrs. M. A. Newell, Port Deposit.
Thomas B. Mackall, Baltimore.
De Courcy W. Thom, Queenstown.

MASSACHUSETTS

The Free Public Library Commission was created in 1890 to encourage the establishment of libraries by direct aid, and to give advice relating to the maintenance and administration of libraries.

Direct Aid. The law of 1890 authorized the Commission to give each town $100 worth of books upon the establishment of a library in accordance with an earlier act relating to the election, powers, and duties of trustees of free libraries. In 1890, 103 towns were without a free public library. In 1904, every town in the state enjoyed the privileges of a library.

In 1892, an act was passed authorizing the Commission to give $100 worth of books to those towns of less than $600,000 valuation, which had established libraries previous to 1890.

To still further aid the poorer towns, the Commission was authorized in 1900 to give an additional $100 worth of books to the towns of less than $600,000 valuation. This grant was usually made in two installments.

To continue service by the Commission to the smaller

libraries, an act was passed in 1906 whereby the Commission might annually expend a sum not exceeding $2,000 in aid of free libraries especially in towns the valuation of which does not exceed $600,000. This law is more elastic than the previous ones, and "aid may include the furnishing of books in small quantities, visits to libraries, the instruction of librarians, and such other means of encouraging and stimulating the small libraries as said commissioners shall deem advisable."

An act of 1910 provides that "the Board of Free Public Library Commissioners shall appoint an agent, with the consent of the Governor, for a period not exceeding five years"; also, that "the Board may annually expend not more than $3,000 for clerical assistance and for other necessary expenses." The salary of the agent is not included in this amount.

Advisory Aid. In addition to the service rendered without compensation by the individual members of the Commission, a board of advisory visitors was organized in 1908, the members of which visit without compensation the small libraries, and report to the Commission the conditions which they find and make recommendations. In this way the "personal touch" has reached most of the smaller towns and many of the larger ones. Twenty-one members served on the board of advisory visitors last year.

Publications:
Annual reports, 1891-date.

Members of the Commission:
Charles F. D. Belden, State Librarian, Boston, Chairman.
Miss Elizabeth P. Sohier, Beverly.
Mr. Hiller C. Wellman, Springfield.
Miss Anna M. Bancroft, Hopedale.
Mr. Frank H. Howes, Newton.

Agent of the Commission:
Miss Zaidee M. Brown, State Library, Boston.

⟩ MICHIGAN

The Board of Library Commissioners encourages the establishment of town libraries by means of the system of registered libraries and works in cooperation with the Department of Public Instruction, the county commissioners of schools, the women's clubs and the county organizers of village and rural libraries. The board employs no assistants, but its work is done in connection with that of the State Library.

Instruction. In 1908, the first session of the Summer School for library training was held at the State Library. The course was free to those holding library positions in Michigan, or under appointment to such positions, and offered elementary instruction on technical subjects, designed to meet the needs of librarians of the smaller libraries. Work with children was made a special feature of this session. A five weeks' course including twenty-two lectures was given by Miss Effie L. Power. For use in this work the Commission obtained a library of 500 v., chosen by Miss Power, as a first selection of children's books for a small public library. The list has been printed by the Commission.

A six weeks' course in library methods has been established in connection with the summer sessions of the three normal schools at Kalamazoo, Marquette and Mt. Pleasant. The two courses into which the work was divided are as follows: Course I designed for teachers having no libraries to administer, included no technical instruction, but laid special emphasis on book selection, care of books, children's books and reading, story telling, etc. Course II, for teachers having school libraries in charge, included technical instruction and practice work in accessioning, classifying and cataloging, in addition to work along the lines given in Course I.

Through the efforts of the State Board of Library Commissioners a library section was embodied in the program of the Michigan State Teachers' Association in 1907. At a meeting of the Upper Peninsula Educational Association, held in Negaunee October 14, 1910 a library section was added to that body. Exhibits of library utilities and books and examples of the loan collection of pictures are displayed at the annual meetings of these associations.

Organizing. In April 1907, a county organizer was appointed to carry on library work on educational lines. Visits have been made to the more isolated portions of the state, and library matters have been presented at state and local teachers' associations, teachers' institutes, farmers' institutes and the state fair.

Assistants are sent out from the State Library to assist small libraries in accessioning, classification and cataloging.

Direct Aid. Under the registration plan any library which is free to the public and which has on its shelves 100 books, not counting government and state documents, may borrow from the Board of Library Commissioners 100 books to be kept six months, when upon a further purchase of books, another loan will be made, equal to the number purchased. This loan applies to township, district and school libraries, if free to the public.

Traveling Libraries. The traveling libraries are under the direction of the state librarian, and are loaned to towns and villages upon application of a group of 20 or 25 taxpayers. Farming communities may apply under the following organizations: granges, farmers' clubs, women's clubs, Epworth Leagues and similar organizations and any society organized for the purpose of study. A yearly fee of $5.00 pays the transportation both ways on four libraries, $1.25 pays the transportation both ways on one library. The regular libraries are made up in sets of 50 volumes for general reading. These may be kept three months and an extension of three months is allowed. To aid the club women of the state, special libraries of books made up on the programs of club work are prepared. They are loaned under the association application.

Legislative Reference Department. A Legislative Reference Department was established in the State Library in 1907. The first work of the department was collecting information in regard to the constitutions of the various states to aid in the work of preparing a new constitution.

Publications:
  Annual reports, 1900-date (1904 o. p.).
  Books for libraries (Reprint of A. L. A. Book-list).
  How shall I catalog my library? (Reprint).
  How to start a library.
  Legislative history of Michigan libraries.
  State aid to libraries.
  Women's clubs and free public libraries.
  List of books for school libraries, grades 1-8.
  List of books for High School libraries, 1909.
  500 children's books for a library.
  Annotated list of reference books for school and public
    libraries, 1910.

Members of the Commission:
  Henry Nelson Loud, President, Au Sable.
  Mrs. Mary C. Spencer, State Librarian, Secretary,
    Lansing.
  David E. Heineman, Detroit.
  Henry R. Pattengill, Lansing.
  Frederick J. Baldwin, Coral.

MINNESOTA

The Minnesota Public Library Commission was established in 1899 to encourage the establishment of libraries in all communities able to support them, to give advice and instruction to those in charge of public libraries already established and to maintain a system of free traveling libraries.

Advisory Work. The Commission endeavors to awaken interest in towns where no libraries exist, through correspondence, printed matter, personal visits, or public meetings for discussion of the library question; gives advice to all towns which are attempting to start libraries, regarding laws and methods of organization, selection of books, furniture and supplies; visits libraries already established to confer with the librarian and library board regarding methods of work and plans for further development; assists in planning library buildings; distributes the A. L. A. Booklist and other aids in book selection to librarians and members of book committees, and also compiles lists for purchase upon special request from individual libraries.

Instruction. The Commission conducts a six-weeks' course in library methods at the University of Minnesota, as a department of the University Summer School. The course is open only to those having library positions or who are under definite appointments to such positions, and includes classification, cataloging, administration, book-selection and buying, reference work, children's work, and all business records necessary in a small library. Further instruction is given by the Commission organizer to each individual librarian in her own library.

In addition to the publications of the Commission, other library literature including the A. L. A. tracts and handbooks is sent out as required.

Beginning in 1909, the Commission has conducted a series of round table meetings each year at convenient points throughout the state, to bring together a group of librarians and trustees for informal conference concerning the problems of every day work. Library interests are also presented at the annual and district meetings of the State Federation of Women's Clubs.

Organizing. When a library is opened for the first time, the Commission sends an organizer to classify the books, start the accession-record and shelf-list, install a proper charging system, and teach the librarian how to keep the necessary records. When the librarian has had summer school training, further assistance is rendered in cataloging. All but local expenses are paid by the Commission, but not more than three weeks time is given to one library.

Institution Libraries. Since 1909, the Commission has included in its field of activity the libraries in the state correctional and charitable institutions. These libraries are visited frequently by the Commission organizer, and assistance is given as needed in classification, cataloging and book selection. The librarians in charge of each institution send monthly reports to the Library Commission, copies of which are submitted to the State Board of Control. Traveling libraries of books carefully selected for this purpose are loaned to the hospitals for the insane.

Traveling Libraries. Through the traveling libraries, the Commission furnishes books to communities having no library facilities and strengthens the resources of the small public libraries with limited book funds, especially in collections for children and in foreign languages, special books and reference aid to students.

The regular traveling libraries are in fixed collections and include 50 volumes for small towns and villages, 25 volumes of general reading for rural communities, 25 volumes of children's books, 25 volumes in Finnish, French, German, Norwegian and Swedish, the "Farmers' library" consisting of 25 books on agriculture and 25 for general reading. These are loaned to any community on application of ten taxpayers, or board of library directors or Farmers' club for Farmers' library. A fee of $1.00 for 50 English books, 50 cents for 25 English books and $1.00 for 25 foreign books is charged. The Commission pays transportation charges.

To adapt the fixed collections to the needs of each community, extra books are added as needed. All requests for books other than fiction are considered and included if possible, and groups of six books on agriculture or in Finnish, French, German, Norwegian and Swedish are added without extra charge.

Home libraries made up of from 10 to 12 volumes are

loaned to individuals living in communities so isolated that a local library association cannot be formed.

The Commission has a large general collection from which libraries for study clubs are made up, covering a wide range of subject and comprising the best books obtainable in the various fields of study. The club libraries contain enough books to cover the subject studied and the number sent varies accordingly. Pictures, stereoscopic views, pamphlets and folios of magazine articles are added when needed to complete the library. These are loaned for a fee of $1.00 in addition to which the club pays the transportation charges both ways. The libraries may be kept for the period of the club year.

This collection also provides books for students pursuing University Extension courses, teachers studying for professional state certificates and material for club and debate loans. Individual loans are sent on application endorsed by district school officers, and the books are sent singly or in small groups for a period of one month for transportation charges only.

' Reference work is a growing feature of work of the traveling libraries, and requests · are received in large numbers from debating societies, teachers, students and librarians for loans on special subjects. Such aid is supplied from the general collection of books, from the magazines on file in the clearing house, or from the larger public libraries by inter-library loans.

Traveling library stations are visited by the librarian as opportunity affords; especially for the purpose of re-establishing stations which have been abandoned and locating libraries in new communities. The traveling library idea is presented at farmers' institutes, teachers' meetings, and club meetings and is further advertised with excellent results through the coöperation of the Extension Division of the Department of Agriculture of the University, by means of articles in their farm papers, and exhibits at the county fairs.

Periodical Exchange. Through the clearing house for periodicals, the Commission assists the public

libraries of the state to complete their files of reference magazines. From the collection of magazines on hand, reference
material is supplied for school debates and study clubs. Il-
lustrated popular magazines not valuable for reference work
are sent to railroad and lumber camps.

School Libraries. The Commission gives advice to
school libraries through correspondence, assists in organizing
such libraries whenever possible, and encourages coöperation between school and public libraries.

In 1909, the Commission revised the Catalog for Public
School Libraries issued by the Department of Public Instruction, and prepared a supplement to this catalog the following year. The *Teachers' assistant,* a selected list from
the school catalog, grades 1 to 5, was published to aid
teachers in rural schools in selection of books. This has
been widely distributed to teachers through the county superintendents of schools.

At the meeting of the State Educational Association in
1910, the Commission held an exhibit including the books
listed on the *Teachers' assistant* and showing other aids in
book selection, and library methods for school libraries. A
representative of the Commission is also sent to the meetings
of each district teachers' association, for the purpose of encouraging better correlation of school libraries and public
libraries.

Publications:
    Biennial reports, 1900- date.
    Publication No. 1, Minnesota library laws, November
       1903.
    Library laws, 1907 (revised).
    Publication No. 2, Public documents in the small library,
       March, 1904.
    Library notes and news, December, 1904- date.
    Leaflets:
       Free traveling libraries.
       —Rules for circulation.
       —Farmers' library.

—Finding lists—Books on agriculture.

— — Household economics.

— — Teachers' library.

Teachers' assistant, a list for rural schools, grades 1 to 5.

Members of the Commission:

Cyrus Northrop, President of the University of Minnesota, Minneapolis.

C. G. Schulz, State Superintendent of Public Instruction, St. Paul.

Warren Upham, Secretary, Minnesota Historical Society, St. Paul.

Miss Margaret J. Evans, Chairman, Northfield.

Miss Gratia A. Countryman, Minneapolis.

Executive Staff:

Miss Clara F. Baldwin, Secretary, The Capitol, St. Paul.

Miss Martha Wilson, Librarian.

Miss Miriam E. Carey, Organizer.

Miss Mary P. Pringle, Assistant.

MISSOURI

The Missouri Library Commission was established by the Legislature of 1907, and was organized October 15, 1907, at which time a secretary was elected to take active charge. The Commission consists of five members, three of whom are appointed by the governor; the State Superintendent of Schools and the President of the State University complete the membership. The Commission is authorized to give advice to all school, free and other public libraries, and to all communities which may propose to establish them; it may receive gifts of money, books or other property; operate a system of traveling libraries; and in general aid in the development of libraries throughout the state.

Legislative. The general assembly of 1909 passed a bill, (Mo. Doc. H. B. 173) creating a General Assembly Library to consist chiefly of the Legislative journals and state documents; but opening the door to progressive reference work for the Legislature. The Library thus collected is to be supervised by the Secretary of the Library Commission under the direction of the House and Senate during Sessions, and to be at other times in charge of the Library Commission alone.

Co-operative Work. Institutes for elementary library teaching have been held for two successive years, (1908-1909) in conjunction with the State Library Association.

As chairman of the Department of Libraries of the Missouri State Teachers' Association, the secretary has arranged programs for representation of library themes at three annual meetings of the teachers. In 1910, the subject "The library as a practical aid to the teacher," was ably discussed by Mr. A. E. Bostwick of St. Louis in an address before the General Session, and the section meeting was held simply for interchange of experience.

Organizing. In June 1910, real field work was begun under Miss Mary P. Farr; during the last seven months of the year, five counties were thoroughly canvassed, and much special work was done with the small libraries of the state.

Traveling Libraries. Fixed Groups 164 are now in use; these contain from 30-50 volumes each. The policy of duplicating groups has been abandoned as tending to reduce elasticity in replacing wornout volumes. General loan collection has been increased by 100 odd in the classes of Agriculture and Home Economics, and many volumes have been circulated through the co-operation of the Farmers' Institute lecturer. Loans from the general shelves were sent to 50 different points in the state during September, October and November of 1910; the number of books in each loan varies from 1 volume to 30 volumes.

Picture Collection. In 1910, five hundred unmounted photographs were purchased for free circulation among the libraries and clubs of the State. They will be mounted to make local exhibition easy and loss difficult.

Publications:
Traveling libraries, what they are and how to secure
them.
Annual report, 1907-date.
Traveling library book-lists.

Members of the Commission:
J. P. Green, Liberty, President.
Miss Adelaide J. Thompson, Jefferson City.
Arthur E. Bostwick, St. Louis.
A. Ross Hill, President University of Missouri, Colum-
bia.
H. A. Gass, State Supt. of Public Schools, Jefferson City.

Executive Staff:
Miss Elizabeth B. Wales, Secretary, Jefferson City.
Miss Mary P. Farr, Organizer.

NEBRASKA

The Public Library Commission was established in 1901,
chiefly for the encouragement of the establishment of libraries, and the improvement of those already established,
with the traveling library as one of the means to this end.

Advisory Work. The Commission gives advice and
suggestions on library matters by personal visits of the secretary, correspondence and the distribution of literature. Lists
of books for purchase are recommended by the Commission,
and the A. L. A. Book-list is sent to every library in the
state.

Organizing. Assistance in organizing is rendered to
small public libraries without charge.

Instruction. The secretary of the Commission
gives instruction to individual librarians in their own libra-

ries. In 1906, a correspondence course was instituted; a course of work in elementary form, with lessons sent to the office of the Commission for revision.

Traveling Libraries. The general traveling libraries are composed of from 40 to 50 volumes of miscellaneons books for adults and children. At the request of the borrowers other books are included on special subjects, children's books and books of general reading when the majority of readers are adults. In addition to the general libraries there are several school libraries containing books for children only, books of general interest and for supplementary reading. Libraries are loaned to any community, upon payment of transportation charges.

From the general loan collection, books on special subjects are loaned to study clubs, teachers, schools and individuals.

School Libraries. The Commission has done much voluntary work in behalf of school libraries. There is no provision made in the school library law for the method of selection and purchase of books, but the Commission has printed a list of books suitable for a school library, and teachers and directors are urged to buy from this list. Many talks have been given by the secretary at teachers' institutes and normal schools and correspondence on the subject of book selection is a feature.

Publications:
    Biennial reports, 1902- date.
    Circular of information.
    Farm circular No. 1, January, 1906.
    How to start a library.
    Library day circular, October, 1905. o. p.
    List of books for school libraries.
    Nebraska library bulletin, February, 1906- date.

Members of the Commission:
    F. L. Haller, President, Omaha.
    S. Avery, Chancellor of the University of Nebraska, Lincoln.

E. C. Bishop, State Superintendent of Public Instruction, Lincoln.

H. C. Lindsay, State Librarian, Lincoln.

Dr. Walter K. Jewett, Librarian of the University of Nebraska, Lincoln.

Executive Staff:

Miss Charlotte Templeton, Secretary, Lincoln.

Miss Guess Humphrey, Librarian.

New Hampshire

The board of trustees of the State Library supersedes the Board of Library Commissioners, assuming all its powers and duties. These are to give advice to public libraries as to selection of books, maintenance and administration, and to expend the grant of $100 for books to each town complying with the necessary conditions.

Advisory Work. The state librarian as representative of the trustees, does much voluntary advisory work through correspondence and library meetings. As the law does not provide for supervisory powers, all this work is suggestive only.

Organizing. New libraries in towns not already having a public library are organized with state aid and under the supervision of the trustees of the State Library.

Direct Aid. The state gives $100 worth of books to each library upon its establishment in towns not already having public libraries.

Documents. The State Library receives the surplus copies of all state publications and is authorized to dispose of them by sale or exchange or otherwise for the benefit of the library. The distribution to the public libraries of the state is made by the secretary of state before the surplus is turned over to the State Library.

Members of the Commission:
William D. Chandler, Chairman, Concord.
William F. Whitcher, Haverhill.
William J. Starr, Manchester.

Executive Officer:
Arthur H. Chase, State Librarian, Secretary, Concord.

New Jersey

The Public Library Commission assists public libraries by giving advice and personal assistance in organization, distributes state aid to libraries, and has charge of the system of traveling libraries, and the libraries in the penal institutions.

Advisory Work. The organizer and other representatives of the Commission visit towns to confer with the librarian, to meet with library boards, to present the library question at popular meetings or before the city council and to address Women's clubs. Special assistance has been given in book-selection by distributing the A. L. A. Book-list and other lists published by different libraries and commissions, and also by revision of lists for individual libraries and making out lists.

Instruction. The Summer School of elementary library science is held at Asbury Park each year. The coming Spring the Commission will hold a week's institute, this to be in the nature of advanced work for students of the school and such other people in the state as may desire it. The program will consist of lectures by some one of national reputation on some of the larger phases of library work, and round table discussions of actual problems which have confronted librarians. These round tables will be conducted by authorities in each line, one being devoted to cataloging, one to reference work, etc. The organizers have coöperated with the New Jersey Library Association in two meetings and have held conferences and round tables in various places for librarians in different districts. A correspondence course in library economy has been carried on for the benefit of those librarians who could not attend the school. The plan has been tried with success of taking librarians and assistants into the State Library for two or more weeks to give them an idea of the work as a whole.

Organizing. The organizer visits libraries to assist the local librarian in the work of organizing or reörganizing, spending as much time in each place as is necessary to teach the librarian how to continue the work.

Direct Aid. $100 is given to each library having less than 5,000 volumes, upon its establishment under municipal control.

Traveling Libraries. The traveling libraries originally loaned by the State Library were placed in the hands of the Commission in 1904. The arrangement of the libraries has been so changed that instead of being made up of collections of fifty books on varied subjects, not subject to change, the books are chosen to suit the one who applies. Traveling libraries are loaned to any community upon application of ten taxpayers, and to any public library upon application of the trustees. An annual fee of $1.00 is charged to cover cost of transportation.

Talks on traveling library work have been made to farmers' granges, and the Commission has placed the libraries and aroused interest in rural communities with the assistance of the State Grange of Patrons of Husbandry.

The Commission has charge of the system of traveling libraries for the state and county penal institutions. These consist of groups sent to each institution made up of a varying number of books to fit the number of inmates in the prisons or jails or reformatories.

Besides the collections sent out special loans of books for study or research, are made to individuals or to groups of people, the books often being borrowed from larger libraries for this purpose.

The two organizers of the Commission are on the staff of lecturers for the Farmer's institutes and teachers' county institutes.

Members of the Commission:
   W. C. Kimball, Passaic, chairman.
   M. Taylor Pyne, Princeton.
   Dr. E. C. Richardson, Princeton.
   Dr. Everett T. Tomlinson, Elizabeth.
   Howard M. Cooper, Camden.

Executive Staff:
   Henry C. Buchanan, Secretary, Trenton.
   Miss Sarah B. Askew, Organizer.
   Miss Edna B. Pratt, Organizer.

New York

The Division of Educational Extension of the New York State Education Department, under supervision of the Director of the State Library, has in charge all the library interests of the state.

Advisory Work. The work of supervising and promoting the organization of public libraries passes under the hands of the Division of Educational Extension and each registered library is visited officially every year. This is the most important work of the division. Much study has been given to library buildings, and plans are suggested and revised. Annual lists of best books are issued by the State Library.

Instruction. The New York State Library School is under the care of the Education Department and the Director of the State Library. A six weeks' summer school is also held. The division has coöperated with the New York Library Association in holding local library institutes, emphasizing instruction in practical library work.

In 1910, library round table meetings were held in thirty-one places, each bringing together a small group of librarians for informal discussion and comparison of views and experiences. This plan will be continued.

Organizing. There are two state organizers who give their time to the libraries, remaining not more than two weeks in one place. Their services are in demand for months in advance. In each case the library served pays all expenses of the organizer while with them, and it is expected that others besides the librarian will take part in the work and learn library methods and ideals from their visitor.

In addition to the organizing work done by special invitation, brief calls are made on many other libraries; the organizers hold round table meetings with groups of librarians and visit teachers, study clubs and institutes for farmers' wives and coöperate with any movement for the promotion of good reading.

Direct Aid. Five dollars to $100 each year may be paid to each registered free library for buying approved books on condition that an equal sum be raised locally for the same purpose.

Traveling Libraries. Libraries for general reading containing a fixed proportion of books on the various subjects are lent to any community. Each group contains 25, 50 or 100 volumes, some including only older, standard books and others the more recent publications. Children's books are in separate groups of twenty-five volumes. A set of annotated lists showing the contents of each library is supplied on request. In addition to the fixed groups, there is a large additional collection of books from which selections may be made. This includes maps and charts but not school text-books, dictionaries or cyclopedias. The catalog of this collection in not in print, but lists of approved books will be lent to borrowers on request. Selections are made as far as possible from these lists, but other books will be furnished if approved.

Libraries on special subjects and in some cases the libraries for general reading are selected from the miscellaneous collection.

Traveling libraries may be lent to:

(1)   Any institution under state supervision on application of its responsible officers.

(2)   Any registered study club or extension center on application of the secretary and the guaranty of a real estate owner.

(3)   Any community without a public library, on application of five resident taxpayers.

(4)   Any club, grange, church, summer school, business corporation or other recorded organization needing books for reading or study, on application of the responsible officer and guaranty of a real estate owner.

No fee is charged for the first 25 volumes where books are available to all the members of the community. When more than 25 volumes are ordered a fee of 50 cents is charged for each additional 25 volumes.

For study clubs, granges, private institutions, etc., the fee is $2 for 25 volumes and $1 for each additional 25 volumes sent in the same shipment.

Transportation charges to and from the nearest railroad, boat or stage office are in all cases paid by the State. Local cartage is paid by the borrower.

Libraries are lent for six months, but schools and registered study clubs whose courses of study last longer than six months are permitted to retain their libraries as late as June 1 of each year.

The Division also encourages work among literary organizations by fixing a standard for registry. Assistance is given in planning courses of study and by lending traveling libraries. The requirements for registry are:

(1)   Five or more members.

(2)   An annual report on official blanks to be transmitted before July 1 of each year.

(3) A course of study approved by the Division of Educational Extension. The primary requisite for such approval is that the subject be sufficiently limited in scope to permit of its intelligent study within the time allotted, which must be not less than ten weeks.

The house library of ten volumes lent for three months for a fee of $1.00, covering transportation both ways, is sent to any household in New York not having convenient free public library privileges. The application must be signed by some real estate owner who guarantees the return of the books in accordance with the rules and to make good any losses or injuries beyond reasonable wear. These house libraries are made up to suit each individual case.

Publications:
Annual report. (in Report of Director of State Library.)
New York Libraries, bulletin of 32 pages, issued quarterly.
Tentative list of 500 to 1,000 volumes of preceding year.
Annotated list of 250 best books of preceding year.
Bulletin of traveling libraries.
Bulletin of library building plans.
Directions for the librarian of a small library.
Buying list of books for small libraries.

Staff of Division of Educational Extension:
Wm. R. Eastman, Chief of Division, Albany.
Asa Wynkoop, Inspector of Public Libraries.
Miss Anna R. Phelps, Organizer.
Miss Caroline Webster, Organizer.
Miss Grace L. Betteridge, Assistant in charge of traveling libraries and study clubs.
Charles F. Porter, Assistant.
Miss Lilian Callahan, Assistant.

New York State Library School:
James I. Wyer, Jr., Director of State Library, Director.
Frank K. Walter, Vice Director.
Miss Katherine Dame, Instructor.
Miss E. M. Sanderson, Registrar.

North Carolina

The North Carolina Library Commission was created by the General Assembly of 1909 and active work was begun September 15 of the same year. The Commission consists of five members, two of whom are appointed by the North Carolina Library Association and one by the Governor; the State Librarian and the Superintendent of Public Instruction are members ex-officio.

The Commission aids in organizing new libraries and in improving those already organized; it gives advice and assistance to all libraries in the state and to all communities which may propose to establish libraries as to the selection of books, cataloging, maintenance and other details of library management; and it maintains a periodical exchange and a clearing house for state reports. The Commission is authorized to establish and maintain a system of traveling libraries, but owing to lack of funds this work has not been undertaken. An effort will be made to secure an apporpriation for traveling libraries from the next General Assembly.

Instruction. In addition to the instruction given in the Commission's office and on personal visits, the Commission conducts a summer school for library training as a regular department of the University of North Carolina Summer School, and in connection with the University Library. The course covers a period of six weeks and consists of special lectures on books as tools and on the use of a library for the general students, and of technical instruction in classification, cataloging, book selection and buying, reference work, etc. for librarians, and for teachers who are in charge of school libraries.

The *North Carolina Library Bulletin,* issued quarterly, is published for the benefit of librarians, trustees, and all interested in library extension work. Other library literature, including the A. L. A. handbooks on Essentials in library administration and Why do we need a public library is distributed as occasion arises.

Periodical Exchange. The periodical file, containing the lists of magazines which the various libraries have for sale or exchange and of those which they wish to procure, enables the Commission to notify the librarians when the wants or duplicates of one library are matched by those of another. Terms and details are arranged by the libraries making the exchange and the magazines are sent direct from one library to another. The part of the Commission in the transaction is merely to serve as a bureau of information.

State Reports. The Commission has established a clearing house for the reports issued by state officers. Until this was done there had never been a center to which surplus reports of the various departments could be sent and to which requests from students and libraries both within and without the state could be referred.

School Libraries. The development of school libraries is a special feature of the work of the North Carolina Library Commission. It has established a close connection with the schools by giving advice on the care and use of school libraries, assistance in starting the necessary records and help in the selection and purchase of books. A bulletin on school libraries, prepared by the secretary of the Commission, has been published and distributed by the Superintendent of Public Instruction to all schools in the state. Other literature on the subject is distributed by the Commission and talks are given at teachers' meetings to arouse the interest of superintendents and teachers in the building up of good school libraries. A special effort is made to bring the public schools and the public libraries into close coöperation. The summer school affords an excellent opportunity for emphasizing the importance of such coöperation.

Publications:
North Carolina Library Bulletin, December 1909 to date.
First biennial report, 1909-1910.
Circular no. 1—The public library.

Members of the Commission:
Louis R. Wilson, Chairman.
Mrs. Sol Weil, Vice-Chairman.
Charles Lee Smith, Treasurer.
J. Y. Joyner.
Miles O. Sherrill.
Executive Officer:
Miss Minnie W. Leatherman, Secretary, Raleigh.

NORTH DAKOTA

The legislature of 1907 created a Public Library Commission consisting of three members; the president of the North Dakota Library Association and the Superintendent of Public Instruction, ex-officio, and one member to be appointed by the governor.

The Legislature of 1909 amended this law adding two members to the Commission, the secretary of the State Historical Society, ex-officio and one member to be appointed by the governor.

It is the duty of the Commission to circulate traveling libraries, to give advice and instruction upon any matter pertaining to the organization, maintenance or administration of libraries, to encourage the formation of libraries where none exist, to keep statistics of the free public libraries of North Dakota and to maintain an educational reference library and a legislative reference bureau for the information and assistance of the members of the legislative assembly.

Advisory Work. The Commission promotes library interest in the state by correspondence, by contributions to newspapers and by sending a worker to assist in organizing libraries. It helps in planning library buildings, in selecting and purchasing books, in securing trained librarians and gives advice on any subject pertaining to library work.

Traveling Libraries. The system of traveling libraries formerly circulated by the State Superintendent of

Public Instruction is now in the care of the Library Commission. These libraries are in fixed groups and contain books for general reading and study for adults and children. They are sent for six months to communities, libraries, schools, colleges, universities, study clubs, and library associations free of cost except for transportation, and under such rules and regulations as protect the property of the state and best increase the efficiency of the service.

In 1910 especial attention has been given to the formation of Farmers' libraries. These are fixed groups of twelve to fifteen technical books on farming and are sent on application of three farmers who agree to circulate them in their vicinity.

Educational Reference Library. From the general loan collection of about three thousand books on special subjects, study clubs, teachers, schools, debating societies, and individuals may borrow books free of cost except for payment of transportation both ways.

Legislative Reference Work. The Legislature of 1907 provided for the maintenance of a legislative reference bureau as a branch of the work of the Commission. The active organization of this department was begun in 1908 by the librarian and director. The work of collecting data on political, legal and economic questions has been vigorously continued ever since. It was found during the session of 1909 that a bureau of this kind can be of much service to members of the legislature and the department proved popular with members of both houses. The aim is to put within convenient reach of the legislator, in classified and condensed form, such information as will enable him to know the economic conditions in other states, the laws as there in force and as they actually meet the conditions that called for their enactment. Books, reports, pamphlets and clippings from newspapers, and periodicals on various subjects of state interest have been collected in the library, together with comparative law briefs and digests of interest to different members of the legislature and state officials.

All legislative bills introduced in the last three sessions have been filed and carefully indexed.

Publications:
Laws of North Dakota relating to Free Public Libraries and the Public Library Commission, 1909.
North Dakota Public Library Commission.
Legislative Reference Library.
Biennial report, 1907-08.
Suggestive list of books for public school libraries, 1909.
Facts about traveling libraries, 1909.
New Year Greetings, 1909.
Free books, 1910.
Permanent state tax commissions, 1910.

Members of the Commission:
Dr. O. G. Libby, Grand Forks, Secretary of State Historical Society, ex-officio.
E. J. Taylor, Bismarck, Superintendent of Public Instruction, ex-ofncio.
Dr. Max Batt, Fargo, President North Dakota Library Association, ex-officio.
A. E. Sheets, Lakota.
Mrs. Clara L. Darrow, Fargo.

Executive Staff:
Mrs. Minnie Clarke Budlong, Secretary and director, Bismarck.
Sveinbjorn Johnson, Legislative Reference Librarian.

OHIO

The first Board of Library Commissioners, under the present law, was appointed April 22, 1896.

The Commission has entire charge of the State Library and has done much to popularize that institution and extend its sphere of activity. It is now open to all citizens.   Its service through the mails is rapidly extending. It is not only a reference library for state officials and members of the General Assembly, but also the free public library of the entire state.

Advisory Work. The Commission is by law authorized to give advice in relation to "the maintenance and administration" of public libraries. This authority has been liberally interpreted and substantial assistance has been given to those seeking such aid. The law was amended in 1906 and the employment of a library organizer is now authorized.

Organizing. At the 1908 session of the General Assembly there was made an appropriation of $3,000, which covers all expenses of the department of library organization. The Board of Commissioners have specified the duties of the organizer as follows:

To give aid and counsel by correspondence and personal visits to cities, towns and communities proposing to establish libraries.

To assist in reorganizing old libraries according to modern methods, which will insure greater efficiency and the best results.

To gather statistics of Ohio libraries for the use of this Commission and the guidance and information of trustees and others.

To give advice and assistance in planning library buildings and collect material on this subject for the use of the library board.

To prepare an annual report to the Board of Library Commissioners on the general library condition of the state.

Within the past two years the library organizer and an assistant have been at work in the discharge of these duties. Visits have been made to public libraries, aid has been given in the establishment of new libraries, and a number of libraries have been partially or completely reorganized by the introduction of modern methods. Many district meetings have been held in different sections of the state. These have been well attended by librarians and those interested in library work.

Monthly Bulletin. In April, 1905, the Commission commenced the publication of a monthly bulletin. This is devoted chiefly to lists of important current additions to the State Library. Some numbers cover special topics, as *Initiative and referendum, Primary elections, Free railway passes, Capital punishment, Ohio's state flower, Ohio's jewels, Seal of Ohio and the Northwest territory.* Recently a considerable portion of the space in the Bulletin has been devoted to district library meetings and other news items relating to the work of the different departments of the State Library.

Traveling Libraries. The traveling library is administered as a department of the State Library. The so-called "flexible" system, as distinguished from "fixed collections" has been used since the issue of the first traveling library in Ohio. Collections varying in number of volumes are sent to women's clubs, schools, granges, public libraries, independent study clubs, religious organizations, men's clubs, and the W. C. T. U. These are loaned for three months, with privilege of renewal, the transportation both ways being paid by the borrowers. The traveling library department issues small collections of books on agriculture, not exceeding eight volumes each to individual patrons, and other books are loaned to individuals for a period of four weeks.

Legislative Reference Department. The General Assembly in 1910 enacted a law authorizing the board of library commissioners to establish, in connection with the Ohio State Library, a "legislative reference and information department" and appropriated $3,000 for its support. The work of the new department has been inaugurated and those in charge hope to render substantial service at the coming session of the General Assembly. It is their aim to popularize this service and extend it to a wider patronage through the public libraries of the state.

Publications:
Publications of the state of Ohio, 1896.
Lafayette day leaflet, 1899.

Newspapers and periodicals in Ohio State Library, other
libraries of the state, and lists of Ohio newspapers in
the Library of Congress and the Library of the Historical Society of Wisconsin, 1902.

Sketches of Ohio libraries, 1902.

Early newspapers in Ohio, 1902.

Duplicate magazines in Ohio libraries, 1904.

Monthly bulletin. June, 1905- date.

Initiative and referendum, 1907.

Ohio emblems and monuments, 1907.

Books of interest to farmers. 1908.

The children's library. 1908.

The library movement in Ohio. 1909.

Ohio canals.

Board of Library Commissioners:
J. F. McGrew, Springfield.
John McSweeney, Wooster.
Frank N. Sweitzer, Canton.

Executive Staff:
C. B. Galbreath, State Librarian and Secretary, Colum-
bus.
Mary E. Downey, Organizer.
Sabra W. Vought, Assistant Organizer.
Mrs. Ida K. Galbreath, Supt. of Traveling Library Dept.
George H. Edge, Assistant, Legislative Reference Dept.

OREGON

The Oregon Library Commission is authorized by law
to give advice to all schools, free and other public libraries,
and to all communities which may propose to establish them,
to maintain a system of traveling libraries, to publish lists
and circulars of information, to conduct a summer school
of library instruction and a clearing house for free gift to
local libraries. Its regular work far exceeds these provisions.

Advisory Work. The Commission works for the establishment of public libraries in localities able to support them, visits libraries for the purpose of giving advice, distributes library literature for use in newspaper articles or meetings for arousing interest in libraries, gives advice and assistance in planning library buildings, helps in book-selection and purchase.

Instruction. A summer library school was conducted by the Commission in 1906, at the State University. A four-weeks' course was given, covering the essentials of technical work, use of reference books, bibliographical aids, and selection of books. Since that time no session has been held, as the number of small libraries in the State seems not to justify the effort and expense, and Oregon depends upon the schools of neighboring States. The secretary and librarian visit libraries for the purpose of giving instruction and instructional literature is distributed to librarians and trustees.

Organizing. The Commission gives necessary help to small libraries in organizing without charge, in so far as time and funds permit. It is expected that each library shall, if possible, bear the expense.

There are so few public libraries in Oregon and so few towns pay enough to support libraries that the organization work of the Commission is not heavy. The State University, State library, and the State Agricultural College have secured trained librarians and the libraries of these schools have been organized. All state institutions are centered at Salem, the headquarters of the Commission, and a special effort is made to secure and make effective the libraries for the charitable, penal and reformatory institutions.

Traveling Libraries. The Legislature of 1905 authorized the Library Commission to purchase and operate traveling libraries, but no appropriation was made for buying books. The books were bought with gifts from individuals and with subscriptions of associations receiving the libraries. In 1907 the appropriation was increased to allow for purchase of traveling libraries.

Libraries are loaned for six months to villages, schools, granges and country communities upon application of the officers of an association, school or grange, or of ten tax-payers who are required to provide shelving for the books in a suitable place and to pay all transportation charges.

The libraries are made up in groups of fifty volumes each of the best popular books for adults and children. They are shipped in stout cases and are accompanied by catalogs and supplies necessary for keeping records of circulation.

Debate Libraries. In response to requests from debating societies for material upon some special questions, the Commission has made up a number of small libraries for debating societies and for students. The State High School Debating League has been organized as a result of this work; and circulars are printed each year giving lists of questions and suggestions for debaters. These debate libraries contain books, periodical articles, copies of debates in Congress, laws, pamphlets published by societies organized to promote some special reform, briefs and bibliographies. The libraries are limited to public questions of importance, and there is a constant and increasing demand for them, especially from the high schools of the state.

Commencement Parts. A direct outgrowth of the debate libraries is a collection of material for essays, orations and commencement parts. Circulars are annually sent to school principals suggesting subjects for commencement parts, and offering to loan material for preparatory reading.

School Entertainments. A collection of material for special day school programs has also been made, including recitations, dialogues and character plays, and this is very popular for schools and granges.

Grange Libraries. The Commission also makes up libraries for the grange programs, working in coöperation with the State Lecturer and sending to each grange each month a package of material for preparation of the program for the following meeting. There are 127 granges in the state, with an aggregate membership of about 10,000 farmers, and the Commission aims to supply study collections to all of these. The state is divided into nine districts, all of the granges in each district having the same program each month, requiring many duplicate libraries. The program for each meeting contains at least one agricultural topic, and one legislative topic of importance because of initiative legislation or proposed measures for the legislature or for the people.

Teachers' Professional Library. Books especially adapted for the use of teachers in the rural schools have been bought in quantities. These are loaned in groups of ten or fifteen to the county superintendents to distribute among their teachers. The Commission also has a general collection of educational literature which is much used. The plan of concentrating upon the reading of a single simple yet valuable book in each county each year or quarter, has, however, proven more practically benefical than that of loaning generally upon demand.

Rural School Reading. An attempt is made to encourage reading aloud of best books in rural and village schools. The Commission makes loans for this purpose from its model library, and buys certain books in quantity for county. adoption for this purpose, utilizing the collections in different counties each year.

School Libraries. When the law creating the Commission was passed the state school library law was amended, making it obligatory for the Commission to compile a list of books for school libraries and rules for the care of such libraries. The ten cent tax for each child of school age was made mandatory and county superintendents directed to notify the Commission of the amount allowed for each school district. A few counties exceeded the ten-cent limit in 1906; since that time most counties have levied a tax in excess of that required by law, and have sent extra funds raised by the districts. Purchase must be made from the Commission list and through the Commission. This brings very close connection with the schools which report to the Commission upon the books in their libraries and send their selections for annual purchases. It also necessitates work at the teachers' institutes. Regular instruction on the use and care of the school libraries and on the use of the library in teaching geography has been given in nearly every institute in the state and continues annually. The Commission has a series of school library publications to be used at the institutes in making possible systematic use of school libraries. The Commission is also working at institutes to organize teachers' reading circles and to have county adoption annually of one good book for reading aloud in country schools.

Legislative Reference Work. The Commission has no regular department for legislative reference work, but it has attempted to obtain the most important material for the state, and in the six months previous to the Legislature and during the session collect for members much material upon laws and proposed laws. The resources of the Commission have been decidedly limited, but in co-operation with the State Law Library it has been possible to supply most of the material asked for. The work connects with the debate library plan, as much of the material collected for the Legislature is loaned to debating societies between sessions. As Oregon has the initiative plan of law making, this service is extended to all citizens and is especially in demand before general elections. The work with debating societies and granges is largely confined to subjects of importance in local, state, and national legislation.

Libraries and State Institutions. The Commission, at its organization, began some work for the libraries of the state institutions, sending an organizer and making a full report on these libraries to the board in charge of the institutions. The library at the prison has received the most attention.

All state schools and institutions have the privilege of buying books for their libraries from the state school list prepared by the Commission for the public schools of the state, being given the advantage of the school price. A deposit of $50.00, the estimated cost of one fixed traveling library, with the Library Commission entitles the state institutions to the use of the traveling libraries.

The organizer employed by the Library Commission, organized the libraries of the State Normal Schools and instructed the school and the local librarian in library methods. The work was done at the request of the State Normal School Board of Regents and the same methods were adopted in all of the schools.

Documents. A new law passed in 1907 makes the State Library the distributing center for state documents and authorizes the Commission to designate depositories.

Publications:
  School circulars, 1-8.
  Campaign slips, 1-30.
  Reference lists, 1-2.
  Book marks, 1-13.
  Circulars of information, 1-11.
  Home library circulars, 1.
  Library leaflets, 1-2.
  Traveling library lists.
  Biennial reports, 1-2.

Members of the Commission:
  Governor Oswald West, Salem.
  L. A. Alderman, State Superintendent of Public Instruction, Salem.
  P. L. Campbell, President of the University of Oregon.
  Miss Mary F. Isom, Librarian, Library Association, Portland.
  W. B. Ayer, Portland.

Executive Officer:
  Miss Cornelia Marvin, Secretary, Salem.

Pennsylvania

The Pennsylvania Free Library Commission was established in 1899. Under the operation of the law, the work of the Commission divides itself into two parts, that of supervising and encouraging the free library movement through the state, and that of maintaining a system of traveling libraries.

Advisory Work. This department of the work includes the initial effort to promote library work in a new center followed by advice as to library room, service, book selection and technique. Assistance is given by a representative of the Commission in actual work of organization. New libraries are visited often and an especial effort made to maintain a close touch until the library has learned self confidence. All free libraries in the state are visited by a member of the Commission staff to give counsel on any subject which affects the good of the library. Much emphasis is laid on choice of books. The A. L. A. booklist is distributed to free libraries by the Commission and in addition help is given through lists prepared to meet special needs.

Organizing. The Commission gives aid in the technical side of organization to old libraries needing re-organization and to those just starting. When trained service is possible the Commission co-operates with the town in securing the right person for the work. Whenever necessary, the Commission sends a member of its staff to the library in question to teach the person in charge proper methods and possibilities of service by working directly with the librarian. Whenever possible the town is asked to bear the expense of entertainment of the Commission worker.

Traveling Libraries. The traveling libraries are designed to encourage the establishment of permanent libraries wherever possible, and to provide books for localities which cannot support libraries of their own. To this end, libraries are of service in four lines of work:

(1)   Collections of fifty books for general reading, whose purpose is to provide free libraries for communities in which there is no such institution. These are loaned for six months upon application of twelve taxpayers, and payment of a fee of $1.00 to cover cost of transportation both ways.

(2)   Collections on special subjects for study clubs and reading circles. Study clubs are invited to send their programs to the Commission and reference libraries will be made up to cover the subjects. The number of books varies, but all books needed for the proper study of the subjects are included. These libraries are loaned upon application of the officers of the club, for a fee of $1.00 to cover transportation and may be kept until the close of the season's work.

(3)'   Collections are provided for use in connection with the school work through the state. These libraries include fifty volumes, chosen to suit the grade for which they are intended, and designed to arouse interest in school work, as well as to lead the children to an appreciation of the better class of literature. The libraries are loaned upon application of the officers of the School Board for a fee of $1.00, and may be kept until the close of the school year.

(4)   Books are loaned to individuals who are interested in some particular line of study, but are so situated that they cannot secure the books needed. These collections include not more than five works, which may be kept three months. The applicant must be endorsed by a real estate owner, and pay all transportation charges.

Publications:

Annual reports, 1-2.

Bulletin No. 1. Aids in book selection.

Handbook of the Pennsylvania Free Library Commission, 1907.

Pennsylvania Library Notes.

Members of the Commission:

Thomas L. Montgomery, State Librarian, Harrisburg, Secretary, ex-officio.

John Thomson, Free Library of Philadelphia, Treasurer.

Henry Belin, Jr., Scranton.
Horace E. Hayden, Librarian, Wyoming Valley Histori-
cal Society, Wilkes-Barre.
Harrison W. Craver, Pittsburgh.
Henry R. Edmunds, Philadelphia.

Executive Staff:
Robert P. Bliss, Assistant Secretary, Harrisburg.
Miss Helen U. Price, Consulting Librarian.
Miss Anna A. MacDonald, Head of Traveling Libraries.

Rhode Island

Free public libraries, as well as public schools, are under
the general supervision of the State Board of Education. The
State Committee on Libraries, composed of three members of
the Board of Education, performs the duties assigned in some
states to a public library commission. The Committee apportions annual state aid to all free public libraries, and in connection therewith it requires specific and carefully arranged
reports from librarians. It makes rules for the purchase of
books and requires that all lists of books purchased with
state money have its approval. It promotes the organization
of new libraries, gives advice and assistance to librarians,
maintains a system of traveling libraries, and publishes circulars and a quarterly bulletin.

Advisory Work. The Committee, through its agents
and secretary, gives advice on the organization, maintenance
and administration of libraries, participates in local meetings
held for the promotion of library interests, and renders assistance and direction in the establishment of new libraries.
Though not employing a regular library visitor, it engages
experts in library work to visit libraries needing inspection,
to give advice, and to give addresses at library and school
meetings. It subscribes for library journals and book-lists and
distributes them to libraries. Its publications are designed to
give advice and instruction to libraries and library trustees.

Instruction. The Committee has never held library institutes or summer schools for librarians. On request it has occasionally employed a visitor skilled in library work to give personal instruction and guidance in library methods to an inexperienced librarian or to a librarian desiring to know better methods. At teachers' meetings it has provided speakers on methods of coöperation of school and library.

Direct Aid. Beginning in 1875, the State, through the Committee on Libraries, has distributed $174,743.60 among different libraries for the purchase of approved books. It now apportions annually $8,500 among 57 free public libraries, aside from $1,000, appropriated for traveling libraries.

Aid is granted annually to each library as follows: $50 on the first 500 volumes in circulation; $25 every additional 500 volumes; $200 being the maximum appropriation for any one library.

More than half of the appropriation for traveling libraries is expended as direct aid to associations maintaining and circulating libraries.

Traveling Libraries. The system of traveling libraries was established by legislative enactment in 1907 with an annual appropriation of $1,000. It includes (1) traveling libraries circulated by the Committee, (2) traveling or branch libraries distributed to schools with state aid by existing libraries, and (3) traveling libraries maintained and circulated with state aid by associations. There are now 30 libraries of the first class, 19 of the second, 120 of the third, and all number 9,193 volumes, having a circulation for the past year of 25,623 loans.

Books and magazines for the blind are purchased by the Committee and circulated through the instructors of adult blind employed by the Board of Education.

Publications:
Reports, 1875-date.
(Included in Reports of the Board of Education.)
Circulars.

Book lists.
Traveling library lists.
Quarterly Bulletin, 1908-date.

Members of the Committee:
Frank Hill, Chairman, Ashaway.
Frank E. Thompson, Newport.
Samuel W. K. Allen, East Greenwich.

Executive Officer:
Walter E. Ranger, Secretary, State House, Providence.

TENNESSEE

The Tennessee Free Library Commission was established by the Legislature of 1908, and was organized March 1910, at which time a general secretary was elected to take active charge. The Commission consists of five members, the State Superintendent of Public Instruction, the State Librarian, and three persons appointed by the governor for terms of two, four and six years.

The Commission is authorized to give advice to all free public libraries and school libraries, and to all communities which may propose to establish them; it may receive gifts of books or other property; operate a system of traveling libraries; and in general encourage and promote the establishment of libraries throughout the state.

The Commission has no appropriation, but a strong effort will be made to secure one from the next Legislature.

Members of the Commission:
G. H. Baskette, President, Nashville.
Miss Mary Hannah Johnson, Secretary, Nashville.
Mrs. W. D. Beard, Treasurer, Memphis.
R. L. Jones, State Superintendent of Public Instruction, Nashville.
Miss Mary Skeffington, State Librarian, Nashville.

Executive Officer:
Mrs. Pearl Williams Kelley, General Secretary, Nashville.

TEXAS

The act creating the Texas Library and Historical Commission became effective March 19, 1909. It provides for a Commission composed of three members appointed by the Governor and two ex-officio members—the Professor of History in the University of Texas and the Superintendent of Public Instruction.

The duties of the Commission may be grouped as follows: (1) to control and administer the State Library, to collect materials relating to the history of Texas and the adjoining states, to preserve, classify and publish the manuscript archives, to encourage historical work and research; (2) to aid those who are studying the problems to be dealt with by legislation by maintaining in the State Library a section for legislative reference; and (3) to aid and encourage public libraries by giving advice to such persons as contemplate the establishment of public libraries in regard to such matters as the maintenance of public libraries, selection of books, cataloging, and library management.

This comprehensive grant of powers to the Commission is at present greatly restricted for all practical purposes by failure to supply the funds necessary to give them effect.

Publications:
"Texas Libraries," Vol. 1, No. 1 and 2.
Circular No. 1. Law governing the Texas State Library and the Texas Library and Historical Commission.
Circular No. 2. Rules and regulations of the Texas State Library.

Members of the Commission:
Mrs. J. C. Terrell, Fort Worth, Chairman.
Geo. W. Littlefield, Austin.

F. M. Bralley, Austin.
Richard Mays, Corsicana.
E. C. Barker, Austin.

Executive Officer:
E. W. Winkler, State Librarian, Secretary, Austin.

UTAH

The public library movement in Utah was first given authoritative organization and leadership in 1907, when Gov. John C. Cutler, at the suggestion of leading educators, called a state convention to create a live interest in the laws which had been passed some years before, empowering all cities in the state to establish libraries. This convention authorized Superintendent of Public Instruction, A. C. Nelson, to appoint a promoting commission to carry forward the work until the legislature should by law organize a state commission to assume the responsibility.

This first commission was immediately appointed as follows: Prof. Howard R. Driggs, University of Utah, president; Dr. E. G. Gowans, Judge Juvenile Court, vice-president; A. C. Matheson, secretary; E. R. South, treasurer; L. R. Anderson, W. D. Livingston; State Senator John Y. Smith; Prof. Fred W. Reynolds, University of Utah, and Esther Nelson, Librarian University of Utah, members.

The promoting commission carried on a successful campaign of library education, without state funds or other financial help. The members generously gave of their means and time, publishing pamphlets and delivering lectures in about half the cities of the state. The result was a great awakening in library interest.

When the next legislature convened, the promoting commission presented a bill authorizing the appointment of a regular library commission.

The law was passed with some amendments establishing a State Library-Gymnasium Commission of five members to be appointed by the State Board of Education, and to be under its general supervision. Its purpose is "to increase and improve educational advantages of the state by establishing and maintaining free libraries and gymnasiums."

Advisory Work. The new commission began work in May 1907, carrying on the work begun by the promoting commission of stimulating library interest in the various cities and directing them in their efforts. Fully one half of the cities and towns have now taken definite steps toward establishing libraries. The special feature of the work in Utah is the promotion of the public gymnasium with the library. It is believed that through this combination better results will be accomplished by offering to boys and young men opportunities for healthful development of mind and body.

School and Home Libraries. In addition to the great public library work, a decided uplift has also been given within the past two years to the school and home libraries in the state.

A law making it obligatory upon school boards to spend for school libraries fifteen cents per capita annually for each school child, was passed by the last legislature. The books are to be selected from lists made by the State Board of Education. Through this means, the schools are assured the right kind of supplemental books in ample quantity.

The Commission has also done signal service for the home libraries by helping parents in their purchases, by prevailing upon the merchants to carry only choice books at Christmas time.

Publications:
The library-gymnasium movement, 1909.

Members of the Commission:
Dr. Wm. M. Stewart, President.
Dr. George Thomas, Vice-president.
Dr. E. G. Gowans.
Supt. John M. Mills.
Asst. Supt. John S. Welch.

Executive Officer:

Howard R. Driggs, Secretary, University of Utah, Salt
Lake City.

VERMONT

The Board of Library Commissioners, established in
1894, is authorized to give advice to librarians or trustees
of any free library regarding selection of books, cataloging, and any other matters pertaining to the maintenance or
administration of the library; and to distribute state aid to
libraries established under state law. In 1900, an amendment to the law was passed providing for a system of traveling libraries.

In 1908 the library law was repealed and the Board received increased appropriation and larger powers in addition
to that covered by the old law.

Advisory Work. Members of the Commission and
its secretary assist at public meetings for library interests
and in some cases by personal work in a town aid in getting a free library established.

A quarterly bulletin is published to furnish information
bearing upon library work in the state and to supply a medium of communication between the librarians of the state
and the Commission.

Since 1905, the Commission has each year subscribed
for thirty-five copies of *Public Libraries,* and sent the same
free of charge to such libraries in the state as particularly
needed the assistance of such a journal.

To assist librarians in making their selection of books
each public library in the state is supplied with a copy of
the *A. L. A. Book-list.* This list takes the place of the annual lists that were formerly issued by the Commission.

Instruction. Following the plan begun in 1908
the Commission, sometimes in conjunction with the State Library Association, has continued to hold quarterly meetings
at different towns in the state. To these not only librarians
but educators and all interested in libraries and schools have

been invited, and the interest and attendance have been most gratifying, the latter ranging from 50 to over 100. The topics considered have been inspirational rather than technical, and coöperation with schools has been a central theme. In this state school districts were long since abolished and very few schools have libraries so the town library is the center from which schools should be supplied. Emphasis has also been placed on the establishment of branch libraries in towns so situated as to need them, and the circulation of traveling libraries in schools by the local library. Sometimes evening sessions have been held and often the library trustees or association furnish entertainment so these meetings have been delightfully social and informal.

An annual institute of instruction was held at the University of Vermont in Burlington, in July, 1908, at Middlebury College in Middlebury, in July, 1909, and at the Academy in St. Johnsbury in June, 1910, all of which were profitable and well attended. The session of a week was occupied by lessons in book mending and the principles of cataloging and library methods. The course was entirely free, and free rooms and board at reduced rates were provided the first two years. A section in the new law provides that the necessary expenses of a librarian in attendance at such school may be paid by the town, city or incorporated village in which such librarian is employed. Also the Commission is authorized by law to hold such school.

The Commission has the support of practically the entire public press of the state to which it sends all of its publications, and which is supplied regularly by the Publicity committee of the Library Association with items of library interest.

Organizing.   Whenever a town requests aid in cataloging or organizing the Commission pays the traveling expenses of the Secretary who may remain with them not to exceed 4 days, board being furnished by the library. The secretary also orders supplies, and recommends catalogers who may be engaged by the library.

Direct Aid. Upon the establishment of a free public library under state laws any town is entitled to $100 worth of books selected and purchased by the Commission. Under the new law the Commission may also spend a sum not exceeding $1,000 annually for the purchase of books for the annual aid of towns whose grand lists exclusive of polls do not exceed ten thousand dollars, and whose free public libraries are doing efficient work for the public and rendering useful assistance to the public schools. Not more than $100 annually can be given to one town. The policy of the state is to encourage the establishment of the library on the same footing as the public school, that it shall be owned, controlled and supported by the town. This is gradually turning old subscription and association libraries into municipal affairs.

A penalty was also added to the new law to provide for the withdrawal of state books if not properly cared for by a town, and an incorporated village made eligible for state aid.

Traveling Libraries. Three or more citizens may apply for a traveling library and are entitled to the use of such on signing an agreement to pay transportation expenses and to be responsible for the care of the books. "Any local library, literary or other club, agricultural or other society, grange, college, seminary, university extension center, study circle or other association shall, on the same terms and in the discretion of the commissioners have the use of such traveling libraries."

Superintendents of schools and school directors may apply for traveling libraries for use in schools and pay the expenses of transportation of the same from the school funds of their respective towns.

In addition to the general libraries containing from 40 to 50 volumes each, a number of libraries selected especially for school use are loaned to rural schools. To supply the demand of study clubs there are a number of special libraries supplemented by the general reserve library.

For the past two years special attention has been given to the State Institutions,—Reform School, House of Correction, State Prison, and Insane Hospital. These have been visited, the needs of the inmates ascertained and either general or special collections of. books in the traveling libraries sent to them. The results have been good for the Institutions, but hard upon the books and the Board hope to arrange to supply them annually with books that shall remain permanently on their shelves.

Periodical Exchange. To help. public libraries to build up reference collections of magazines, the Commission has established a clearing house for periodicals, on the usual plan, through which many volumes of valuable magazines have been added to the libraries of the state at small expense.

Many more magazines having come in than are called for by the libraries, the Commission has recently donated both sets and odd numbers to the State Institutions, where the sets will be bound and the odd numbers circulated till worn out or cut up for pictures.

Documents. When a town has established a public library, the town may vote to place in the library documents received from the state for the use of the town, with certain exceptions; and the state librarian is directed to deliver to such libraries duplicate documents and volumes published or provided by the state.

Publications:
  Biennial Reports, 1897- date.
  Bulletin, (quarterly) 1905- date.
  Library law, 1908.
  Various circulars of information.
  Traveling library catalogs.

Members of the Commission:
  March M. Wilson, Randolph.
  Mrs. W. P. Smith, St. Johnsbury.

Mrs. C. M. Winslow, Brandon.
Edward M. Goddard, Montpelier.
Miss Fanny B. Fletcher, Proctorsville.

Executive Officer:
Miss Rebecca Wright, Secretary, State House, Montpelier.

Virginia

The Virginia State Library performs many of the functions of a library commission, in that it has charge of the system of traveling libraries, and endeavors in every way possible to advance library interests in general in the state.

Traveling Libraries. In 1906, the General Assembly appropriated $7,500.00 for inaugurating the system of traveling libraries, and gave $1,800.00 a year for 1908 and 1909 for maintaining it.

The libraries consist of fixed collections, numbering from 25 to 50 books. These collections are sent, without charge, on application of ten taxpayers who have formed a local library association by electing a president and librarian. The librarian agrees to abide by all the rules of the State Library regarding the circulation of the books and keeping of records and to return the books at the end of six months. There are three classes of traveling libraries, namely, the libraries for adult readers (called citizens' or general traveling libraries), libraries for the use of pupils of the public schools, and special collections. In addition to the books in the fixed collections, there are about 600 volumes from which selection may be made.

Publications:
Annual report of the State Librarian.

Members of the State Library Board:
Armistead C. Gordon, Chairman, Staunton.
S. S. P. Patteson, Richmond.
John W. Fishburne, Charlottesville.
Theodore S. Garnett, Norfolk.
Edmund Pendleton, Richmond.

Executive Staff:
H. R. McIlwaine, State Librarian, Richmond.
G. C. Moseley, Chief, Division of Traveling Libraries.

WASHINGTON

The State Library Commission consists of the Governor, the judges of the Supreme Court, and the Attorney General, and was created by the law of 1903 to have charge of the State Library and all its departments. In addition an advisory board was created which consists of the Superintendent of Public Instruction and four persons appointed by the Governor, one of whom shall be a person recommended by the Washington State Historical Society, and one of whom shall be a person recommended by the State Federation of Women's clubs. The advisory board is directed by the law to give particular attention to the building up of a state historical department and a system of traveling libraries, and to give advice and counsel to all free libraries in the state, regarding the best means of establishment and administration.

Advisory Work. Under the law of 1903, the Advisory Board of the State Library shall give advice and counsel to all free libraries in the state, and to all communities which may propose to establish them, as to the best means of establishing and administering such libraries, the selection of good books, cataloging and other details of library management. The *A. L. A. Book-list* is distributed to public libraries, as are also all the reports and public documents of the state.

Instruction. A six-weeks' summer school is conducted at the University of Washington under the supervision of the librarian of the University.

Direct Aid. The law of 1903 authorizes the state to give direct financial aid to public libraries under the control of the Library Commission, but no appropriation has yet been made for the purpose.

Traveling Libraries. The traveling library of Washington was started by the State Federation of Women's Clubs, and turned over to the State Library Commission on its establishment in 1901. In 1903, when the Commission was reorganized, the traveling libraries were made a department of the State Library. By the law of 1907, the traveling library work is placed in the hands of a Superintendent of Traveling Libraries, appointed by the Commission but independent of the State Library.

The libraries are sent to any community upon the application of three responsible persons, and upon the payment of transportation charges. A special effort has been made to reach study clubs, who are urged to send in programs. Lists of books in the State Library, bearing on the subjects pursued, are sent to the clubs to make their selection. The only expense to the clubs is the transportation fee and any number of books desired are supplied.

Periodical Clearing House. Volumes and single numbers of magazines are supplied to public libraries on the usual exchange plan.

Documents. The State Library has full control of the distribution of state documents. A legislative reference department has been organized on the same plan as that in Wisconsin.

Publications:
    Biennial reports, 1904, 1906.
    Library laws of Washington, 1903.

Washington Library Association Bulletin (quarterly).
Check-List of Pacific North West History, 1909.

Members of the Commission:
Governor M. E. Hay.
Attorney-General W. P. Bell.
Supreme Justice Mark A. Fullerton.
Supreme Justice Wallace Mount.
Supreme Justice Ralph O. Dunbar.
Supreme Justice S. J. Chadwick.
Supreme Justice M. F. Gose.
Supreme Justice Herman D. Crow.
Supreme Justice Frank H. Rudkin.
Supreme Justice Geo. E. Morris.
Supreme Justice E. F. Parker.

State Library Advisory Board:
H. B. Dewey, Supt. Public Instruction, ex-officio.
Mrs. Kate Turner Holmes, Seattle, representing Federation of Women's Clubs.
Mr. F. F. Hopper, Tacoma, representing State Historical Society.
W. E. Henry, Seattle, Libu. University of Washington.
Senator J. D. Bassett, Ritzville.

Executive Staff:
J. M. Hitt, State Librarian, Secretary, ex-officio, Olympia.
Miss Josephine Holgate, Assistant Librarian.
Mrs. Lou G. Diven, Superintendent Traveling Library
. Department.

WISCONSIN

The Free Library Commission carries on its work of library extension in Wisconsin through (1) the Instructional Department, which includes the maintenance of the Wisconsin Library School as well as a summer school and various library institutes, (2) the Department of Library Extension and Visitation, which is closely associated with the Instructional Department, (3) the Traveling Library Department, and (4) the Legislative Reference Department, which includes a legislative bill drafting department as well as the legislative reference library.

Advisory Work. In the organization of a new library, the Commission offers such advice and assistance as is needed. A member of the staff may- be sent to advise with the board as to best methods of organization. Frequent visits' are made to the libraries for the purpose of giving aid and counsel in the improvement of methods of work, in planning new branches of service, in choice of books. Much time has been given to the study of library buildings, their planning and equipment, and an excellent collection of photographs and plans has been made, together with specifications, samples, and estimates of cost.

The first *Suggestive list of books* for a small library was published in 1897 and several revised editions of this have been issued since that time. *Buying-lists of recent books* to supplement the *Suggestive list* were issued at frequent intervals, and special bibliographies have also been prepared. The 1905 edition of the *Suggestive list* of books (for adults) was compiled by the Wisconsin Commission and published by the League of Library Commissions. A Suggestive list of books for children has been prepared by the Commission and is now being published by the League. Since the *A. L. A. Book-list* began publication in 1905, the *Buying-lists* have been discontinued.

Instruction. The Commission gives instruction in library methods through a library school, through library institutes, and through personal visits to librarians in their libraries.

A summer library school was instituted in 1895. In 1899 the school was made a permanent institution of the Commission, with an annual elementary course of eight weeks which was later changed to six weeks. It is conducted in connection with the summer school of the University of Wis-

consin.   The instruction given includes cataloging, classification, reference work, book buying and book selection,
children's literature, work with children in the library and
school, and instruction in technical work and business methods suited to the small library.   In 1902, 1904, 1906, 1908, a
supplementary course of several weeks was conducted, intended for those who had completed the elementary training, and offering courses in the study of books and the inspirational side of library work.

A permanent library school offering a course of one year
was opened in September, 1906.   The course of instruction
covers the fundamental principles of library work in all its
branches, bibliographical, technical, and administrative, developed on practical rather than theoretical lines.   It includes
twenty-six weeks of actual curriculum work with two months
(February and March) devoted to field practice in the libraries of the state under the supervision of members of
the teaching staff.

The establishment of a course offered jointly by the University of Wisconsin and the Library School marked an important epoch in the history of the school.   During the
freshman and sophomore years, students in the University
follow the usual college courses, electing those calculated to
make the best foundation for library work; at the end of the
sophomore year they take the entrance examinations of the
Library School.   If they are admitted to the Library School,
the University in recognition of the school's standards of
scholarship, grants twenty hours (five hours each semester)
of credit toward the A. B. degree for work done in the Library School in the junior and senior years.

Library institutes have been held in various parts of
the state to give elementary instruction to librarians who
cannot come to the library school.   These institutes also
serve as conferences for librarians who have had more or
less training, and afford opportunity for the comparative
study of methods and an interchange of ideas.

Instruction is given in the small libraries to the librarians
individually while the organization of the library progresses,
and every subsequent visit of the members of the Commis-

sion staff brings some addition to the librarian's stock of library knowledge and enthusiasm. It is the aim of the Commission to visit every library in the state at least once each year.

The Commission distributes annually to the libraries of the state, much library literature of an instructional nature including aids in book selection, the A. L. A. Booklist, special lists, etc. Since January, 1905, the *Wisconsin Library Bulletin,* published bimonthly, has been sent to every library in the state. This contains helpful articles and suggestions on practical topics, answers to questions arising in library work, and lists of a bibliographical nature, and constitutes a medium for exchange of ideas between the Commission and the libraries as well as between the different libraries themselves.

Organizing. The Commission aids in classifying and cataloging the books, installing a charging system and putting the library on a thorough working and business basis. If the library is in a large town with generous support, the Commission gives advice and counsel, assists in finding trained librarians, oversees the organization generally, but does not do the actual work. In cases where less funds are available, the Commission furnishes the services but expects the library to bear part of the expense; while in the case of small libraries, the Commission gives the time of the organizer.

Traveling Libraries. The Commission maintains a system of traveling libraries. These are sent to farming communities and to villages too small to support public libraries; to larger villages and towns for the purpose of encouraging the establishment of local libraries; to villages and towns already maintaining public libraries, but whose book funds are insufficient for the frequent purchases of books necessary to sustain public interest; to study clubs not having access to public libraries offering adequate service; and to public libraries with large numbers of German, Scandinavian or Polish patrons, libraries made up of books in their languages. The study libraries are retained as long as the club pursues the subject they cover; the other series are kept six months, when exchange is made. The English libraries contain from 50 to 60 of the best popular books in fiction, history, travel, biography, science and literature for adults and children. The study libraries vary greatly in number of books, and are sometimes supplemented by magazines and pamphlets. They are accompanied with outlines and programs. The German, Scandinavian and Polish libraries contain 35-40 books. These libraries are loaned to public libraries for a rental fee of $7 a year, there being a semi-annual exchange of boxes. Foreign groups comprising ten books each are added to the English traveling libraries sent to communities where a foreign-born element can be served. There are collections in German, Polish, Norwegian, Swedish, Bohemian, Yiddish and French.

"Town" traveling libraries, comprising 100 English books each, are intended for the larger villages and smaller cities financially unable to maintain a public library, but too populous to remain satisfied with a traveling library of the usual size. Upon payment of $12 a year, the Commission agrees to supply 100 books which are exchanged semi-annually for other collections of like character. Transportation charges are paid by the local station. A library organization is effected in each place, and frequently a reading-room is opened. in connection with the traveling library. These "Town" libraries are also sent upon the same terms to small public libraries to supplement their small collections of books.

The Commission also has a few groups composed of fifty attractive books largely the best new fiction to meet the demand from those small libraries which wish to keep up to date in books but have insufficient funds. These "new book" libraries are sent out in the same way that the "town" libraries are handled at a cost of $10 per year.

The traveling library stations are visited from time to time that the Commission may keep in touch with the communities served and that direct knowledge may be gained of the individual condition and needs of each station.

Many of the counties of the state have established systems of traveling libraries under an enabling law which permits counties to appropriate $500 for the initial establishment of the system, together with $50 for salary of librarian and $25 for traveling expenses, the sum of $200 annually with salary for librarian and expenses being allowed in subsequent years.

Periodical Exchange. The Commission operates a clearing house for magazines with the purpose of building up reference collections of bound periodicals in the public libraries of the state, and supplying current topics' material for clubs. It also sends large quantities of the popular magazines to lumber camps, etc.

Documents. Each established library of over 1,000 volumes is entitled to one copy of all documents published by the state. The Commission designates such libraries as depositories of state documents and prepares lists for the use of the State Superintendent of Public Property. The Commission has also compiled a check-list of state documents and will publish supplementary lists as they are required. Printed catalog cards of state documents are prepared by the Commission to be distributed to public libraries and to the various departments of the state.

Legislative Reference Department. In 1901, the Legislature authorized the Commission to conduct a legislative reference room, and to gather and index for the use of members of the Legislature and the executive officers of the state such reports, bills, documents and other material from Wisconsin and other states as would aid them in their official duties. This department aims to build up a working library of present-day subjects, so that the history of legislation and all possible material on economic problems may be readily available as each question arises. The work has already had a decided effect upon good legislation in Wisconsin and is very popular with all members of the Legislature. In 1907 a bill-drafting department was organized to assist the members of the legislature in putting into proper form their ideas as to needed legislation. The appropriation of $1,500 for the first year, has now been increased to $15,000 a year.

Publications:
American social questions, nos. 1-6.
Anniversaries and holidays.
Biennial report, v. 8, 1910.
Bulletin (bi-monthly) January, 1905 to date.
Check list of journals and public documents of Wisconsin, 1903.

Circulars of information:
1 Establishing a library, first steps.
2 How to secure a traveling library.
3 Suggestions for library rules and regulations.
4 Magazines for the small library.
5 Campaigning for a public library.
6 Legislative reference department.
7 Traveling libraries in Wisconsin.
Comparative legislation bulletins, nos. 1-21.
Instructional department pamphlets:
1 Wisconsin library school, 1909-10.
2 Short course, library school, 1910.
3 Picture collections in small libraries.
4 Supplementary course, library school, 1908.
5 Commercial geography.
6 Books on missions.
7 How to care for books in a library.

Traveling library circulars:
1 Traveling libraries for public libraries.
2 Traveling libraries for communities without public libraries.

Miscellaneous pamphlets:
Laws of Wisconsin relating to free public libraries and the Free library commission 1905 (1911 in preparation).
Library extension, by Edward A. Birge, 1905.
One hundred popular German books.
Some Wisconsin library buildings.
Study outlines, nos. 1-23.

Members of the Commission:

James M. Pereles, Milwaukee.

Reuben G. Thwaites, Secretary State Historical Society, Madison.

Mrs. Charles S. Morris, Berlin.

Charles R. Van Hise, President University of Wisconsin, Madison.

Charles P. Cary, Superintendent of Public Instruction, Madison.

Executive Staff:

Matthew S. Dudgeon, Secretary, and Director of Library School, Madison.

Charles McCarthy, Chief of Legislative Reference Department.

Miss L. E. Stearns, Chief of Traveling Library Department.

Miss Mary Emogene Hazeltine, Chief of Instructional Department and Preceptor of Library School.

Miss Ethel F. McCollough, Instructor Library School.

Miss Helen T. Kennedy, Instructor Library School.

Miss Helen Turvill, Instructor Library School.

Miss Mary Carpenter, Instructor Library School.

Miss Ono M. Imhoff, Cataloger Legislative Reference Department.

Mrs. Anna L. Mayers, Executive Clerk.

Name of Commission	Date estab.	Executive Offi
*Alabama Dept. of Archives and History:—		
Division of Library Extension........	1907	Thomas M. Owen, Di
*California State Library..................	1903	James L. Gillis, State
Colorado Board of Library Commissioners...	1899	C. R. Dudley, Presid
Colorado Traveling Library Commission.....	1903	Carrie M. Cushing, T
*Connecticut Public Library Committee.....	1893	Mrs. Belle Holcomb Librar
*Delaware State Library Commission........	1901	H. Ridgely Harringto
*Georgia Library Commission..............;	1897	Mrs. Percival Sneed,
Idaho State Library Commission...........:	1901	S. Belle Chamberlain,
*Illinois Library Extension Commission......	1909	Eugenia Allin, Orga
*Indiana Public Library Commission........	1899	Carl H. Milam, Secy.
*Iowa Library Commission..................	1900	Alice S. Tyler, Secy..
Kansas Traveling Libraries Commission.....	1899	Mrs. Adrian Greene,
*Kentucky Library Commission..............	1910	Fannie C. Rawson, S
Maine Library Commission..................	1899	H. C. Prince, Secy...
Maryland State Library Commission.........	1901	Bernard C. Steiner,
*Massachusetts Free Pub. Lib. Commission	1890	Zaidee M. Brown, A
*Michigan State Board of Lib. Commissioners	1899	Mrs. Mary C. Spence
*Minnesota Public Library Commission......	1899	Clara F. Baldwin, Se
*Missouri Library Commission..............	1907	Elizabeth B. Wales,
*Nebraska Public Library Commission......	1901	Charlotte Templeton,
New Hampshire Public Library Commission.	1891	Arthur H. Chase, Sec
*New Jersey Public Library Commission.....	1899	Henry C. Buchanan,
*New York State Education Dept:—		
Division of Educational Extension.....	1892	W. R. Eastman, Chie
*North Carolina Library Commission........	1909	Minnie W. Leatherm
*North Dakota Public Library Commission..	1907	Mrs. Minnie C. Budl and
*Ohio Board of Library Commissioners......	1896	C. B. Galbreath, Secy
*Oregon Library Commission................	1905	Cornelia Marvin, Sec
*Pennsylvania Free Library Commission.....	1899	T. L. Montgomery,
*Rhode Island Dept. of Education:—		
State Committee on Libraries..........	1907	Walter E. Ranger, S
*Tennessee Free Library Commission........	1909	Mrs. Pearl W. Kelley
Texas Library and Historical Commission...	1909	E. W. Winkler, Secy.
Utah Library—Gymnasium Commission......	1909	Howard R. Driggs,
*Vermont Board of Library Commissioners..	1894	Rebecca Wright, Sec
Virginia State Library.....................	1906	H. R. McIlwaine, Lib'
*Washington State Library Commission.....	1901	J. M. Hitt, Secy.....
*Wisconsin Free Library Commission.......	1895	Matthew S. Dudgeon,

		Board of Trustees of State Library.
5	Governor	
5	Governor	Nominated by Colorado Federation of Women's Clubs.
1	State Board of Educ.	
5	Governor	State libn., .secretary ex-officio.
3	Governor	Atty.-gen'l, sec. of state, supt. of pub. instruction and pres. of State University.
	Commissioners of State Library	State libn., member ex-officio.
4	Governor	
5	Governor	State libn., supt. of pub. instruction, pres. of State Univ., members ex-officio, 2 appointees to be women.
3	Directors of State Lib.	State libn., ex-officio ch'n., pres. Kansas State social science fed. of clubs, member ex-officio.
5	Governor	
4	Governor	State libn., secretary ex-officio.
2	Governor	State libn., supt. of pub. instruction and libn. of Enoch Pratt library, members ex-officio. 2 appointees to be women.
5	Governor	State libn., chairman ex-officio.
4	Governor	State libn., secretary ex-officio.
6	Governor	Pres. of State Univ., supt. of pub. instruction, sec. of State Hist. Soc., members ex-officio.
6	Governor	State supt. of schools, pres. of State Univ., members ex-officio.
5	Governor	State libn., supt of pub. instruction, chancellor and libn. of State Univ., members ex-officio.
3	Governor	Board of Trustees of State Library.
5	Governor	
5	Governor & N. C. Lib. Assn.	State libn., supt. of pub. instruction, members ex-officio.
5	Governor	Supt. of pub. instruction, pres. of N. D. Lib. Assn., sec. of State Hist. Soc., members ex-officio.
6	Governor	Commission has control of State Library.
5	Governor	Governor, supt. of pub. instruction, pres. of State Univ., and libn. of Portland Lib. Assn., members ex-officio.
5	Governor	State libn., secretary ex-officio.
		3 members of State Bd. of Educ. compose the committee, commissioner of pub. schools, secretary ex-officio.
6	Governor	State libn., supt. of pub. instruction, members ex-officio.
	Governor	Supt. of pub. instruction, prof. of hist. in Univ. of Texas, members ex-officio.
	State Board of Educ.	
5	Governor	
		Board of Trustees of State Library.
		Governor, atty.-gen'l and judges of Supreme Court compose commission; advisory bd. of 5, consists of supt. of pub. instruction, and 4 appointees of governor.
5	Governor	Pres. of State Univ., supt. of pub. instruction and sec. of State Hist. Soc., members ex-officio.